THE COMPLETE
DREAM
DICTIONARY

A Bedside Guide to Knowing
What Your Dreams Mean

Trish and Rob MacGregor

Adams Media
Avon, Massachusetts

Published by Adams Media, an F+W Publications Company
57 Littlefield Street
Avon, MA 02322

ISBN: 1-59337-109-8

Printed in Canada

J I H G F E D C B A

Library of Congress Cataloging-in-Publication Data
MacGregor, T. J.
The complete dream dictionary / Trish and Rob MacGregor.
p.   cm.
ISBN 1-59337-109-8
1. Dream interpretation—Dictionaries. 2. Dreams—Dictionaries.
I. MacGregor, Rob. II. Title.
BF1091.M312 2004
154.6'3'03--dc22
2004004816

This publication is designed to provide accurate and authoritative information with regard to the subject matter covered. It is sold with the understanding that the publisher is not engaged in rendering legal, accounting, or other professional advice. If legal advice or other expert assistance is required, the services of a competent professional person should be sought.
—From a *Declaration of Principles* jointly adopted by a Committee of the American Bar Association and a Committee of Publishers and Associations

Contains material adapted and abridged from *The Everything® Dreams Book* by Trish and Rob MacGregor, ©1998, Adams Media Corporation. Some additional information adapted from *The Everything® Psychic Book* by Michael R. Hathaway, D.C.H., ©2003, Adams Media Corporation; *The Everything® Wicca and Witchcraft Book* by Marian Singer, ©2002, Adams Media Corporation; *The Everything® Divining the Future Book* by Jenni Kosarin, ©2003, Adams Media Corporation; and *The Everything® Meditation Book* by Rosemary Clark, ©2003, Adams Media Corporation.

Many of the designations used by manufacturers and sellers to distinguish their products are claimed as trademarks. Where those designations appear in this book and Adams Media was aware of a trademark claim, the designations have been printed with initial capital letters.

This book is available at quantity discounts for bulk purchases.
For information, please call 1-800-872-5627.

Visit our home page at *www.adamsmedia.com*.

Contents

Introduction

Throughout history, human beings have wondered about the meaning of dreams. In many ancient cultures, dreams were thought to have prophetic meaning. Still other societies thought that you could control "real life" events through your dreams. In more modern times, Sigmund Freud, the father of psychoanalysis, suggested that dreams are simply a means through which unconscious thoughts manifest themselves. But what, exactly, are dreams, and what can they tell you about your life? This book will help you to explore the origins of your dreams, how and why you dream, what common dream symbols generally mean, and what significance they hold for you in a more specific sense.

If you are intrigued by what your dreams really mean, you are probably eager to dive into this dictionary. Often, upon initial reflection, your dreams probably seem incredibly bizarre. Why do you dream about losing your teeth, or about being naked in public? What does being in class or failing tests symbolize, and why do you dream of spiders all the time? Typical dream symbols such as these have a variety of common meanings, which you will learn about in this dream dictionary. However, these interpretations are meant to serve only as a springboard for reflection, so that you can examine all the clues and then derive further meaning from the specific circumstances of your own dream.

For example, you might have a dream that includes a bird in it. When you look up "bird," you will read that generally, these creatures are a positive sign. And while this might be helpful, it can also sometimes be frustrating. What if the bird in your dream turned into your mother? Or what if it was talking to you? Or what if it was impersonating Mick Jagger? These radically different dreams can't possibly have only one interpretation.

So what are you supposed to do? The key to dream interpretation lies in psychology. Don't worry—you don't have to have a doctorate in the subject. What you do need is to be able to use your instinct and your common sense. As you work with this book, read the introductory chapters first and try to develop your own personal insights into what the common symbols in your dreams mean. Through the various examples, you can begin to build a working glossary of your own personal definitions. Then, as you use this dictionary, the explanations given will add insight to your own interpretations. And when there are certain symbols in your dreams that continue to puzzle you, this glossary will also help to trigger ideas that "click" for you.

When using the dictionary, be careful not to rely on it totally to interpret your dreams. Ultimately, when it comes to dream symbols, there are no equivocally universal rules or meanings, so keep that in mind as you explore your dreams. Dream dictionaries do help by providing hints at the meaning of symbols that appear in your dreams, but, especially when the elements of the dream are personal, the meanings given might not totally resonate for you. Remember, no dream dictionary in the world is going to tell you the meaning of that dream you just had about your Uncle Bill, whom you haven't seen for twelve years. These are the times when you're going to have to follow your instincts and look for meanings of your own, based on the circumstances of your dream.

Also bear in mind that while some dreams might be a literal message of something that is about to happen to you, others often provide a symbolic message. Pay attention to key elements and symbols, but also take note of other details—the colors, the vividness, the action, and anything unusual that stands out. If you dream of a particular animal, for instance, associate it with situations and conditions in your life, institutions that you deal with, or people you know well. These types of details will all provide context clues to the meaning of your dreams.

Above all, as you first begin to explore your dreams, be patient. Know that it might take awhile for you to develop your dream recall technique, and that the way you are able to recall your own dreams will be different from anyone else's technique. For that matter, so is the information you receive in your dreams. Dream recall is like learning any other skill: The more you practice, the more you will learn to recall and interpret what you are experiencing through your dreams.

Ultimately, dreams are about soul-searching. You can ignore things that happen in your everyday life, but during your sleep your fears, desires, and even psychic visions come to pay a friendly visit—or to scare the heck out of you—and you don't have a whole lot of control over it.

By examining your dreams, deciphering and decoding them piece by piece, you can accomplish one monumental task—the task of understanding your life and yourself on a deeper level. The better you get at interpreting your own dreams, the more they will help you to fathom the feelings, situations, events, and actions of your waking life. This will help you to gain the knowledge and the confidence you need to find better, healthier solutions to the problems you face. In this sense, your dreams truly are the mirror image of your soul, and therein lies their deepest value.

Chapter 1

The History of Dreams

Through the centuries, our collective dream consciousness has been spurred by support from a variety of great thinkers and leaders, including Julius Caesar, Socrates, Hippocrates, and St. John. As diverse as all of these individuals were, they held one thing in common: All were strong proponents of finding visions of the future, seeking creative inspiration, and exploring much more in dreams.

As a culture, the Greeks were great lovers of dreaming. From the socio-economic hub of Athens, ideas about dreaming traveled around the ancient world. As these ideas spread among kings, merchants, and commoners alike, each culture and society added a little more lore to the blend until some symbols emerged as archetypal.

(You'll learn more on the meaning of archetypes in dreams later in this book.)

Dream interpretation was by no means limited to the Western world, however. The Eastern traditions favored dream oracles as well. While the oracles at Delphi and Epidaurus were speaking about dreams, Japanese Buddhists were conducting similar rites. In Japanese culture, dreams had a very honorable advocate in the emperor, who was given the duty of sleeping in a special chamber to receive regular missives from the Spirit through his dreams.

🔅 The Origins of Dream Interpretation

Spiritual dreaming and dream interpretation are certainly not recent traditions. The earliest written dream keys date back to 1350 B.C. in Egypt, indicating a much earlier oral history. One dream key, *Oneirocritica* (*The Interpretation of Dreams*), written by Artemidorus Daldianus around 140 A.D., became so popular that it was still being printed in the 1700s. ❱

Further, the Egyptian, Mesopotamian, Hittite, Hebrew, Druidical, and Taoist priests and priestesses (just to name a few) regarded dreaming as a suitable way to connect with the Divine. Even St. Augustine and Martin Luther agreed with this concept, as do Native Americans to this day. Humankind has a longstanding tradition of recognizing dreams as spiritual tools, and today, as our modern understanding increases, we still see the spiritual links and continue to explore and understand the emotional and psychological connections as well.

Contemporary Connections

Although through the years interest in dream interpretation waxed and waned with social contrivance, it received a huge boost at the turn of the twentieth century when Carl Jung and Sigmund Freud began writing about dreams. Although the nuances of their individual theories are too complex to boil down into a nutshell, there are a few generalities worth noting for now. Jung believed that our nighttime forays illustrated a vast scope of universal ideas, sometimes gathered from the collective unconscious. Freud, on the other hand, believed that dreams exposed suppressed desires and information hidden in each person's individual subconscious.

But there is even more than all of this to the significance of dreams. They may recount mundane thoughts and actions, reveal what is overlooked or

> **Creative and Inspiring Dreams**
> Some of the world's greatest creative works and inventions have come from the dream state. Albert Einstein literally "dreamed up" his Theory of Relativity—it came to him while he was sleeping. And the English poet Samuel Taylor Coleridge dreamt the idea for the opening lines of his poem *Kubla Khan* after reading about the Mongol emperor right before he dozed off from a sedative. Ideas for great stories, music, and poetry can come through your own dreams, too. They're often sparked from your unconscious mind, usually when you have been thinking about a particular topic or problem. The unconscious mind simply pieces together all the information it has and sends it up to you while you are in your dream state.

ignored, and cast glimpses into the future. They have the power to teach dreamers about human life, interactions, and the way the world works; they also have the power to act as the voice of the Divine or even a reflection of It. Most importantly, perhaps, they teach us about ourselves and also remind us of the power we hold within us, even when we don't realize or understand it.

The Whole Versus the Sum of Its Parts

The Babylonians regarded the whole dream (as opposed to its individual parts) as a message. Assyrians held a completely opposite belief, that each element in a dream has specific meaning or ominous portent. A more accurate stance probably lies somewhere in the middle. The entirety of a dream holds import—its continuity, its feeling, the impressions you are left with upon waking— all of these things are significant. But the details are also meaningful, and sometimes, the human mind leaves integral clues in even the smallest, seemingly insignificant tidbits.

As you begin to consider your dreams, don't feel as if you need to measure them up against each other, compare the vividness of the details, or judge them according to how long or short they are. The length and amount of detail in a dream isn't a terribly important issue. For one thing, time is elusive in the dream world; what appears to be a moment can translate into hours of real time, and vice versa. Also, short dreams with only one or two images can be just as powerful and insightful, if not more so, than lengthy ones that require a lot of sorting to decipher.

With this foundation in mind, remember the following points when attempting to interpret your dreams:

1. Note your first gut feeling about the dream. Don't just brush off first impressions—they're important. Very often, the initial feeling or ideas that come to mind upon waking are on the mark. And if the meaning of the dream seems obvious, it probably is exactly as it seems.

2. Try to interpret any references to obvious internal or external influences, such as something seen on TV or in the newspapers, or obvious personal fantasies and memories. Internal or external influences hold import to a dream. It's possible you could simply be dreaming about those memories or feelings, but it's also likely that those influences hold insight into the situation or question at hand.

3. Look at the dream as a whole. Is there a theme to it? What's the overall setting or sense of atmosphere? Try to see the big picture.

4. Look at the details. Does there seem to be a repeated message? It might come through words, objects, colors, aromas, or symbols that are duplicated or have the same connotation. Alternatively, write down each component and the meaning it has for you, then compare them to the impressions from the whole dream.

5. Consider the dream's patterns, progressions, or cycles. For example, a dream that begins in spring and ends in winter might be connected to the flow of time, the change of seasons, and so on. Patterns often prove important to the overall interpretation.

6. Reflect on the dream. When time allows, think about the dream and all the impressions you've gathered. If you think of new parts of the dream previously forgotten, add those into the process. Make note of any notions that come to you during this re-examination.

Part One

Understanding Dreams

Chapter 2

Sleep Basics

You spend about a third of your life asleep. That means that in a lifespan of seventy-five years, you sleep the equivalent of twenty-five years. To some extent, your social and cultural expectations have influenced your ideas about how much sleep you're supposed to have. While eight hours is considered the average, some people need less, some need more. You might need less sleep when your life is humming along on an even keel, but during periods of illness, stress, depression, pregnancy, or tumultuous change, more sleep might be necessary.

If you're one of those fortunate people who feels fine after six hours of sleep, then it simply means you're a more efficient sleeper. You also have two more hours a day at your disposal.

Dreams make up about 20 percent of your sleeping life, and in an average lifetime, you will experience well over a hundred thousand dreams. And yet, not until fairly recently did science begin to investigate and understand what occurs during sleep, or how and why we dream. When we dream, bits of data from the subconscious, superconscious, and Spirit can filter through because we've slowed down enough to pay attention. As we learn more about dreaming, it is becoming increasingly apparent how important this aspect of sleep is to our psyche—and to our experiences in waking life.

Conscious Versus Unconscious

Since dreaming involves complex interaction among the different levels of mental faculty, it's important to understand what each level is about. The conscious mind is what we are most familiar with. Consciousness is the active awareness of your mental and physical state, with the ability to modify these states. It is your immediate involvement with the present and encompasses the functions of your senses. Sight, hearing, touch, taste, and scent all involve your attention and evoke responses that you might or might not manage according to your will. The waking conscious brings information and challenges to our attention. Associating, recognizing, analyzing, and comparing are all functions on this level.

The unconscious is sometimes called the subconscious, meaning what is below or beneath consciousness. It is a realm to which psychology and religion have given great attention, for good reason. The unconscious stores everything that the waking conscious delegates to the back burner. The unconscious also possesses memories, symbols, feelings, and thoughts that aren't necessarily pertinent to the needs of the here-and-now. Dreams are a manifestation of the power of the unconscious. We typically don't dictate to the unconscious when we will dream, or what we will dream (except in certain, advanced dream-practice, called lucid dreaming, which you will learn more about later on). The unconscious produces activity and information according to its own agenda, which is certainly our agenda, but not in the same terms of our conscious life. When dreaming, we are all subject to the currents of the unconscious mind, and learning to tap into this power can lead us to realizations that we might not encounter in our waking consciousness.

The Superconscious

Different traditions view the superconscious in different ways and call it by different names, but the premise is the same: The superconscious is the intangible, spiritual nature of human existence. It is the self in Jungian psychology, the soul of Christianity, the divine body of mystical traditions, the *atman* in Yoga philosophy, and the Buddha nature in Buddhism. Is this potential accessible to ordinary people? According to both secular and religious meditation traditions, it is the inevitable result of consistent and dedicated practice. Research has also been done in dream work to explore this connection to elements of the superconscious during sleep.

Brain Rhythms

Before delving further into what, exactly, happens when you dream, it's necessary to understand the sleep process and how it is tied to brain rhythms. There are rhythms that are wired into the human body, and their activity during sleep plays an integral role during the dream process. Electrical impulses between nerve cells produce all activity in the brain, the control center of the body. These impulses are measured in hertz, or cycles per second. Researchers have correlated specific states of consciousness with the number of cycles produced by brain waves. Brain waves are grouped into four categories: beta, alpha, theta, and delta. However, current research is refining these categories as scientists learn more about the mind, body, and consciousness.

The Beta State

The beta state, the most active state of the mind, consists of waves of twelve to sixteen cycles per second and is associated with the engaged mind. Speaking, relating to others, learning a new skill—all of these activities fall into the beta state. High beta, with waves of sixteen to thirty-two cycles per second, denotes high emotions, such as fear or excitement. The mind is focused on specifics, situations that might be either desirable or threatening. The super-high beta state, with waves of thirty-five to 150 cycles per second, was only recently discovered.

Alpha State

The alpha state (waves of eight to twelve cycles per second) is a relaxed state of nonarousal. Thinking disturbs the alpha state, but attention is active. Reflection and contemplation are associated with this category. It is the target state of most meditation and biofeedback exercises. At normal range, the human heart produces seventy-two beats per minute. The same rhythm is believed to induce a state of relaxation in alpha state, and if emulated in music, it can be hypnotic.

Theta State

The theta state (waves of four to eight cycles per second) is found in light sleep and deep meditation. This is a "bridge state" between tranquility and drifting into unconsciousness. Daydreams occur here, as well as events in which the person is conscious but unable to recall details.

Delta State

The delta state (which consists of waves of one-half to four cycles per second) is found in deep sleep. This is the lowest cycle observed. In this state, the mind is not attentive to anything in the outside world.

What Happens When You Sleep

In the course of a typical night, you pass through four distinct phases of sleep. These are distinguished by the frequency of brain waves, eye movements, and muscle tension.

In the first stage, the rhythms of the brain shift from beta waves—the brain waves of your normal waking consciousness—to alpha, when brain waves oscillate between eight and twelve cycles per second. At this point, your heart and pulse rates, blood pressure, and body temperature drop slightly, your muscles begin to relax, and you experience drifting sensations. This is the time when hypnogogic images—surreal scenes that usually concern your last thoughts before turning out the light or some facet of your waking life—might flit through your mind. These hypnogogic images are often vivid and psychedelic. Though brief, the images can be as meaningful and significant as longer dreams in deeper stages of sleep.

In stage two you experience a deepening of the drifting sensation as you fall into a light slumber.

The brain wave pattern now registers theta waves, characterized by rapid bursts of brain activity. On an electroencephalogram, these waves appear as spindles and are believed to signify true sleep. Yet, interestingly, people who are awakened during this phase report they weren't asleep, but were "thinking."

☀ Your Sleep Habits

Try to track your sleep habits for two weeks. Create a sleep log for each day, and note the time you went to sleep, approximately how long it took you to fall asleep, the time you woke up, how you felt, whether you were rested, whether you napped in the afternoon that day, and anything else related to your sleep patterns. This will prepare you to work with your dreams. ▶

Most of our dreams occur in stage two. If you watch someone sleeping, you can actually see them dream, because their eyes move back and forth beneath their eyelids. This period of rapid eye movement, or REM, usually lasts for several minutes at a time during the second stage.

Twenty to forty-five minutes after the sleep cycle begins, the spindle pattern of brain waves is replaced by large, slow delta waves. Delta waves indicate the plunge into deeper stages of slumber.

In stage three the EEG consists of 20 to 50 percent delta waves; in stage four the EEG registers more than 50 percent delta waves. People who are awakened from this phase are usually disoriented and want to go back to sleep. There are no eye movements at all. This is the stage where sleepwalking might occur. Delta waves can last from a few seconds to an hour.

Sleep Cycles

During the course of a night's sleep, your body goes through several cycles. For example, in an adult male, the cycles of sleep typically last about ninety minutes and then are reversed. But this time, when you reach the second stage again, your blood pressure rises, your pulse quickens, and your brain waves are similar to those during the waking state. Except for twitches in your fingers and toes, and the movement of your eyes in REM sleep, your body becomes virtually paralyzed. If you are awakened during the REM period, you'll probably remember most of whatever you're dreaming.

This first REM period lasts from five to ten minutes; then you go through the cycles of sleep three or four more times. Each time the REM stage is repeated, it lasts longer and the time that elapses between cycles is considerably shorter. The final REM stage can last up to an hour.

This means that if you sleep seven hours, then half your dreaming time will occur during the last two hours. If you sleep an additional hour, that eighth hour will consist almost entirely of dreaming. This is, however, only an average. People who need less than eight hours of sleep might simply be more efficient sleepers.

Sleep Disturbances

A sleep disturbance doesn't only disrupt your sleep. When you don't sleep well, your dreamtime is shortchanged. If you don't dream as you should, you suffer physically, emotionally, and spiritually. It invariably affects the other areas of your life. How you deal with a sleep disturbance is often just as important as the cause of the disturbance.

According to the American Sleep Association, over forty million people in this country suffer from sleep disorders. If you have chronic sleep problems, don't wait to seek help for your problem. Aside from the lack of sleep itself, an insomniac is robbed of valuable dreamtime that could provide physical, emotional, and spiritual guidance and solutions.

Sleepwalking

Sleepwalking, or somnambulism, occurs when a sleeping person gets up and walks or undertakes another activity, like getting dressed. Sleepwalking is most common in children aged six through twelve and normally occurs during non-REM sleep, early in the night. Some symptoms include open eyes, incomprehensible talking, blank facial expressions, and grogginess or disorientation upon awakening. It is not dangerous to awaken a sleepwalker—in fact, it's a good idea to do so to prevent injury! ❱

Age and Sleep

Age is the most important natural factor that influences sleep. A fetus spends as much as 80 percent of its time in the womb in REM sleep. Before the thirtieth week in utero, nearly *all* of its sleep is REM, which is believed to supply intense stimulation to the central nervous system.

It's unknown whether a fetus's REM sleep involves dreaming. Researchers who believe that the contents of dreams are derived from life argue that a fetus can't possibly be dreaming. But in cultures where reincarnation is an accepted belief system, these REM sleep periods in a fetus might be viewed as dreams from a previous life that are somehow preparing the soul for this life.

In the first few weeks after birth, an infant sleeps about sixteen hours a day and may spend as much as eight to ten hours in REM sleep. This is also the time when the baby's brain grows at a staggering rate. The correlation between these two facts is not random. Some neurophysiologists believe that the internal stimulation of dreams triggers neurological growth in the brain and helps prepare the infant for its waking environment.

By two years of age, the brain of a child has nearly doubled in size. The child is sleeping fewer hours—about thirteen—and is spending less time in REM sleep. By four or five years of age, a child's dream cycles are similar to those of an adult.

If prompted, small children (two to four years of age) will talk about their dreams. In some cultures where dreams are accorded great respect this is a regular part of life, and children are encouraged to remember and discuss their dreams.

The Elderly

By the time you're sixty years old, your sleep cycle is more fragmented and variable than it was when you were forty. While the average night's sleep doesn't change all that much, the time spent in deep sleep does. Since the elderly tend to be lighter sleepers, they are awakened more easily during the night.

Insomnia among the elderly is a pervasive problem. But in many instances, it's the result of lying in bed and, like insomniacs of all ages, worrying about the loss of sleep. This behavior also affects the ability to dream.

A Note on Pregnancy

Even if you have a normal pregnancy, your sleep patterns might change. Early in the last trimester, physical discomforts could awaken you in the middle of the night. Unfortunately, once the baby is born, you will probably get even less sleep.

At that point, you can forget about eight hours of uninterrupted, blissful, dream-filled sleep. In fact, you can forget all your notions about what constitutes sleep. Babies, after all, get hungry about every four hours, and they don't care where the food comes from as long as they're fed.

Since you're sleeping less, you're dreaming less, and you're probably recalling fewer dreams.

However, some women report particularly vivid dreams during pregnancy, especially during the last trimester. These dreams often have to do with the unborn baby and might express the woman's anxieties over the impending labor and delivery. Women who are open to the concept of telepathic communication with their unborn child might even experience dreams in which they're conversing with a small boy or girl.

Chapter 3

Remembering and Cultivating Your Dreams

Everyone dreams, even if they do not remember their dreams in the morning. In fact, dreaming regularly is essential to human psychological stability. Without enough REM sleep, during which dreaming occurs, people can easily begin misinterpreting the real world until daily life becomes just as bad as the nightmares they can't recall having while asleep!

Sometimes, however, dreams are so startling or vivid that you can't help but remember them. Often, these are the times that you wake up with a start during the night. At that time, you might think, "I won't forget this one." Yet, by morning a fog often settles over your memories of the night's "events." By then, you might only recall the flavor of the dream and little else. Or, you might just remember thinking that you weren't going to forget your dream.

Dream Recall

The best way to remember dreams is to record them immediately after they occur. If you don't usually wake up after a dream, try giving yourself a suggestion before you go to sleep that you will wake up following each dream, although it might not be a good idea to do so every night. By doing this, you might reach a point where you can recall four or five—or more—dreams a night.

Jot down your dreams on a bedside pad or record them on a tape. At first, your nighttime scrawls might be virtually indecipherable, but with practice you'll learn to write clearly enough so that you will be able to transcribe the dream into a journal in the morning.

If waking up during the night to record your dreams just isn't for you, the next best time to recall a dream is in the morning before you get up. Experts all seem to agree that how you awaken in the morning is vital to preliminary recall of dreams. Whenever you can dispense with your alarm clock, by all means do so. An alarm intrudes, jerking you from a sound sleep so quickly that your dream tends to fade as soon as you open your eyes.

☀️ How Bright Is Your Dream?

Author William Brugh Joy advises paying particular attention to the lighting in a dream. If a dream is brilliantly colored and vivid, it reflects the superconscious state—the more evolved areas of consciousness. If the light in a dream is soft or shadowy, in sepia tones like an old photograph, or if it's in black and white, Joy says it emanates from less evolved areas of consciousness. Dreams that are even darker originate from the deep unconscious. ▶

To awaken without an alarm, of course, is difficult if you're working a nine-to-five job or have young children. One alternative is to start your dream work on a weekend, when you might be able to sleep later and to wake up without an alarm. Another alternative is to train yourself to wake up without an alarm. This is actually much easier to do than it sounds. Before going to sleep at night, simply give yourself a suggestion to wake up at a particular time, say, ten minutes before your alarm clock goes off. If it doesn't work immediately, keep trying until you feel confident you can eliminate the alarm clock.

Once you wake up, don't open your eyes immediately. Just lie there for a few minutes, retrieving your dream images. If nothing comes to mind, try moving into your favorite sleep position. This might trigger some dream fragment that will expand.

Sometimes it also helps to have reference points to aid you in the recollection of a dream. Quite often, our own thoughts about our dreams are the biggest obstacles to recalling them. Initially, don't try to overanalyze your dream scenario—just write it down as if it were someone else's story. Later, when you interpret the dream, you might find that what seemed silly or outrageous or insignificant has far deeper meaning than you initially realized.

Using a Dream Journal

A dream journal is an integral part of dream exploration. A notebook will do, but a bound journal is even better. Some are specifically designed as dream journals and include a place for the date and time of the dream, the dream itself, and your interpretation.

If your bedside writing isn't clear, transcribe your dreams later into a "permanent" notebook or onto a computer file. Or, if you use a notebook computer, keep it near the bed and type the dreams directly into it when you wake up.

Keep the journal and a penlight nearby—on a nightstand, on the floor, or even under your pillow. If you do jot down your dreams during the night or tape-record them, then set aside a time to transcribe them into your journal.

☀ Dream Overdrive

Retraining yourself to remember more dreams can be tough. But what happens when you are so successful in learning to give yourself suggestions for dreams recall that you can't stop the dam from flowing once it's opened? If you ever find yourself remembering too many dreams and it gets to be overwhelming, you can reverse the dream recall process. Just as you can suggest that your mind remember certain dreams, you can also suggest that you don't want to remember so many of them, to give yourself a break. ▶

When you describe the dream, include as many details as possible. Who, what, where, when, and how act as excellent guidelines when collecting details. Were you alone? If not, who was with you? Friends? Family? Strangers? What activity, if any, were you or the others engaged in? Was it day or night? Dark or light? Where were you? How did the dream strike you? Was it familiar, odd, or pleasant? Also pay attention to how you feel upon awakening.

Here are some reminders for what to include in your daily dream journal:

• **Dream descriptions:** Write down everything you can remember the moment you wake up. To remind yourself, keep the journal and a pen next to your bed.

• **Symbols:** Keep track of your own personal dream symbols, especially those that reoccur periodically.

• **Feelings:** How did you feel in a particular dream? Writing down your feelings may help you make sense of the dream—often the feelings are more important than the dream's plot. When you record a dream, include how you felt upon awakening. Pay attention to your dominant emotion: Is it one of exhilaration, fear, sadness, happiness, or something else?

• **Characters:** Are the people in your dream from your present or past—or are they strangers? If you're always dreaming of people from your distant past, for example, chances are that your unconscious is still trying to figure out events from your earlier life or even childhood.

• **Dream Category:** Categorize each of your dreams. Was it a dream sparked by events in your everyday life, a dream rooted in fear or anxiety, a dream expressing a particular wish or desire, or a dream that seems to be telling you something about the future? (The specific implications of these various types of dreams will be discussed in greater detail later on.) By writing these things down, you'll start noticing patterns that will help you become more aware of your unconscious and how it is assimilating your thoughts.

When attempting to recall dreams, also jot down whatever you were thinking about at the time you went to bed. These details can provide clues to the meaning of your dreams as well. If you jot down your general impressions at first, sometimes, when you go back over the dream, these might help you to remember more details.

Sometimes, you might not remember the specifics of a dream, only that you've dreamed. Then, later, your recollection of the dream is triggered by something in your waking environment. When this happens, be sure to note the event or experience that triggered the recollection, because it can provide vital clues about the dream's meaning or significance.

Keep in mind that if you're not getting enough sleep, recalling your dreams is going to be much more difficult. If you initially have trouble recalling dreams at night, then try recapturing a dream when you wake up from a nap.

⊙ The Benefits of Meditation

Because meditation makes you aware of other states of mind, it can be another means to assist dream recall. By quieting your conscious mind, symbols and images can flow more freely from the intuitive self. The technique you use depends entirely on what feels most natural to you. A walk in the woods or on the beach can serve just as well as ten or twenty minutes of sitting quietly after you wake up. ▶

If you try and try, and yet you still can't remember your dreams, the problem might lie in the "invisible beliefs" that you're holding. Perhaps, in your heart of hearts, you're afraid to remember your dreams. Or you're afraid to know what you dream about. Or maybe you believe your dreams could tell you more than you want to know. Examine your beliefs honestly, and you might be able uncover what's preventing you from remembering your dreams.

🔆 Sandman Visualization

When trying to improve dream recall, it helps to relax your body before you fall asleep. Start by thinking of your entire body as being filled with sand. In your mind's eye, reach down and remove corks from your toes. Let the sand slowly flow out, taking with it your tensions and negativity. As each part of your body "empties," feel it grow light and unburdened. You might even fall asleep during this process; if so, all the better. This visualization helps to unblock a lot of barriers for dreams. ◗

Help Yourself to Remember

The best time to suggest to yourself that you will remember your dreams is in a slightly altered state, because your mind is more open. As you drift to sleep at night, tell yourself that you will recall the most important dream you have. If you have a specific question that you want answered, tell yourself that you'll remember the dream that answers that question. Repeat this request several times as you fall asleep. Make sure that your journal and a pen are within reach.

During quiet moments throughout the day, you should also remind yourself that you're going to remember your dreams. If you have particular questions you want answered, phrase those questions to yourself. Experiment with different methods until you find the one that works best for you. It helps if you sincerely believe you can receive answers through your dreams.

Tap into Your Senses

As you work on improving your own personal dream interpretations, keep in mind that connecting with your senses can help to trigger improved recall. Start by tapping into the sense that resonates most strongly for you. If, for instance, you are a highly visual person, focus on one picture image you remember from your dream, and see if in your mind's eye you can change your view, bringing images closer or moving them back. As you examine these visual elements, try to pause the action you're remembering at various points, so that you can look for things you missed before. If your sense of hearing is particularly strong, focus on the sounds that go with the images in your dreams. After you begin with your most acute sensations, work through all of your sensory recollections, noting other elements, such as textures, temperatures, tastes, and smells. The various emotions connected with these sensations will help you to find greater insight in your dreams.

Dream Incubation

The fact is, whether we remember our dreams or not, we're constantly guided by them. Once you begin to recall dreams with ease, it's possible to request dreams that will guide you and even give you hints of future events on particular issues or dilemmas—a relationship issue, a health matter, a career question, or something else. Or you may simply request a dream that you will remember. The act of asking for a dream, for whatever purpose, is called dream incubation.

This process was popular in many ancient cultures including Mesopotamia, ancient Egypt, Rome, and Greece. People often traveled to temples dedicated to specific gods, where they spent the night in hopes of receiving a dream that would heal, illuminate, guide, and provide solutions. In some temples, priests were available to help seekers interpret their dreams. There were even professional dream seekers, who were hired by people too ill or otherwise unable to travel to the dream temples.

The Method

Today, there may be no recognized dream temples for seekers, but anyone can practice dream incubation in their own home. The first step in dream incubation is knowing what to ask for and considering the things you are concerned about. Then, decide which of these areas you want to focus on.

🔆 Dream Patterns

Even if you wake with no conscious memory of a dream, make a note in your journal about how you feel. Do your dreams occur regularly or sporadically? Do you remember dreams daily, weekly, monthly, or less often than that? Do you have specific dreams for specific moments in your life? Do you dream more when you eat certain foods before you go to bed? Over a period of time, the data you collect will help you establish your sleep and dream patterns. ❭

Some experts recommend writing your request for a dream on a slip of paper and placing it on your nightstand or under your pillow, because by making a ritual our of your request, you are formalizing it. Most of the time, however, a sincere need and intent will suffice. And, of course, you have to remember the dream. But even the need to remember the dream can be included in your request.

Gayle Delaney, in her book *Breakthrough Dreaming*, suggests that you jot down five or ten lines about your request in your dream journal. Then condense this to a phrase or question that states what you want to know. As you fall asleep, repeat this phrase or question to yourself.

Even if you don't remember anything the first time you try this, keep at it. With persistence, you'll recall a dream that addresses your concern. Be aware, however, that sometimes your answers might not be what you bargained for.

Dream Interviews

If you attempt dream recall and incubation, and you reflect on your dream, yet the meaning of a dream continues to evade you, it's a good idea to approach it as if you were being interviewed. This technique is often used by therapists to help the dreamer uncover the meaning of a particular dream or series of dreams. But you don't need a therapist to try the dream interview technique. A trusted friend or a spouse can act as the interviewer or you can act as your own interviewer. Just remember that the dream interviewer should never sway the dreamer. The dreamer should come upon his or her own interpretation naturally, not because someone else's interpretations were suggested.

The first step with this technique is to name your dream. This will help you to distinguish the dream in your journal, and it might also help you

A Brainstorming Exercise

To help you identify areas that you would like to focus on in your dream work, try brainstorming about key elements of your life. Once you recognize them, you'll have a better idea about what to request from your dreaming self.

1. **Consider your relationships:** What are your most intimate relationships generally like? Do you feel good or bad about your relationship with your spouse, significant other, or others who are important in your life? Can you identify any patterns in your relationships with your parents, siblings, other family members, or friends? What would you change, if you could? In a perfect world, what would your relationships be like?

2. **Think about your work and career:** Is there anything you would like to change about your work? How much money would
continued on following page

to pinpoint a major image or symbol. Then, once you've recorded the dream in your journal, run through the details in your mind and highlight the most important items: the setting, time of day, people, emotions, animals or other objects and symbols, and major actions.

(This technique is an expansion of one developed by dream therapist Gayle Delaney and her partner, Loma Flowers, directors of the Delaney and Flowers Center for the Study of Dreams.)

continued from previous page

you like to earn, ideally? What is your ideal job? How do you feel about your boss and other coworkers?

3. **Analyze your health/physical self:** Do you like the way you look and feel? If you could change anything about the way you look, what would it be? How is your health at present? Do you have any chronic problems? Have you been to doctors recently? What is your ideal version of yourself?

4. **Reflect on your spiritual life:** What do you believe in? How do you feel about your spiritual life? How would you like to develop, spiritually?

5. **Explore other thoughts on your life in general:** In six months, where would you would like to be? What about in a year, or in five years? Is there anything you're looking for guidance on?

Once you decide on someone to be the interviewer, work from your list to devise questions. Try to give as much detail in your answers as possible. Be sure either to use a tape recorder or notebook to document the information, so that you can review it later.

Once you become proficient at dream interpretation, the interview technique will become

More Thoughts on Recording Your Dreams

When it comes to understanding and interpreting your dreams, the importance of recording them cannot be stressed enough. This book has already touched on using a dream journal or even a tape recorder. You can also create your own dream dictionary on your computer. Some creative folks even sketch or paint their dreams, because having a visual imagery helps their recall. Regardless of the medium you choose, recording a dream serves several functions. First, it often helps clarify the details of the dream. Second, it allows you to review and interpret those details at a convenient time (instead of trying to figure out interpretations while rushing out the door to work). Third, the meaning of many spiritual dreams (which will be discussed in the chapter on types of dreams) might not become clear for days, weeks, months, even years. Therefore, having a record to look back upon and find the "Aha!" therein is, indeed, of great help. Such illuminating moments will reinforce your faith in the messages your dreams send you and the power within them to help you with daily life.

second nature. You won't have to write out the entire interview or record it, although you might still want to do that with complex dreams.

☀ Children's Dreams

Children's dreams often hold clues to the same anxieties and insecurities that plague their parents. Some kids will talk spontaneously about their dreams; other kids might have to be prodded. But one fact holds true for all kids: If they live in households where dream sharing is simply part of the family routine, they'll be more apt to remember and relate their dreams. ◗

A Quick Review

Before you move on and begin exploring common dream themes, take a few minutes to review some essential guidelines for effective dream recall:

• **Voice what you need or want:** Before you fall asleep at night, state aloud that you would like to remember the most important dreams of the night. If you're trying to find a specific solution to something in particular, then request that an answer come to you in a dream that you'll remember in detail.

• **Back up your request with a gesture:** Things like putting a tape recorder by your bedside or sliding a notebook under your pillow will help to suggest all the more to your mind that you are serious about dream recall. This way, you'll also be ready to record whatever snippets of your dreams you remember immediately when you wake up. You might even jot your request on a page in your dream journal. Date it, and make notes the next day about whether you remembered any dreams. Keep in mind that sometimes, even just the act of trying to write about your dreams when you're sure you haven't remembered any is enough to trigger recall.

• **If you don't succeed at first, keep trying:** Yes, it's a cliché, but it's very true. If you've spent thirty or forty years forgetting the bulk of what goes on while you sleep, then you can bet your dream-recall wheels are rusty. Keep making your requests, and sooner or later, you'll have a powerful, significant dream—and you'll remember the characters, the details, texture, and other nuances vividly.

• **Experiment:** If you're following all of the necessary steps, and yet you still don't seem to be remembering any dreams and your requests don't appear to be working, try sleeping elsewhere for a couple of nights. Sleep on the couch, in a sleeping bag, or even at your parents' place. When you change a familiar habit, it helps to break the rut and new things often unfold.

Chapter 4

Common Dream Associations and Themes

Although each person's experience with dreams is different, there are certain types of dreams and themes that are common. As you continue to work at remembering your dreams, you will begin to recognize the various types of dreams. When you learn how to identify some of these broad dream categories, you'll be able to build a context for your dreams, and this framework will help you to gain insight into their meanings.

Watch for Metaphors, Puns, and Archetypes

Among other things, dreams have a lot to teach us about the relevance of universal symbols. Recognizing metaphors, puns, and archetypes that appear in your dreams is key to inferring their personal meaning. When you recognize a metaphor, a perplexing dream can suddenly crystallize and resonate more clearly. If, for instance, you dream of people who are not in your life anymore, think about what they represent. When someone from your old job was a gossip, and that person appears in your a dream, he or she might symbolize gossip to you.

The same can be true of dreams about celebrities. For example, a dream of Bob Hope bouncing along on a pogo stick and moving off into the distance might at first seem outrageous and nonsensical. But by looking at the elements of the dream in terms of a play on words, the message is revealed: Hope springs eternal.

An archetype is a symbol or theme that rises from a layer of the mind common to all people. In addition to our own personal meanings for the symbols in our dreams, Carl Jung believed that we can identify with collective/universal themes, stories, and characters. Jung called this layer the "collective unconscious" and believed that we each give these symbols and themes our own individual stamp. "I call it 'collective' because, unlike the personal unconscious, it is not made up of individual and more or less unique contents but of those which are universal and of regular occurrence," Jung wrote in *Memories, Dreams, Reflections* and *The Structure and Dynamics of the Psyche*. Jung used the term *amplification* to describe this process of identifying with collective images because he thought of it as expanding details of individual dreams into what he termed a "universal framework."

Archetypes are prevalent in mythology, folklore, and religion. The hero, for instance, is a common theme, from classical mythology (Apollo or Zeus), to modern tales (Luke Skywalker or Harry Potter). You may not consciously recognize an archetype when you encounter it, but it will

Other Sides of Yourself

Remember that you are not the only reflection of yourself in your dreams. We project other sides or aspects of ourselves onto other people, animals, and even inanimate objects in our dreams, because we simply can't play all of our roles at once. This recognition will help you to build a variety of perspectives on your dreams, and it will help you to find different ways of looking at dream situations. In this way, you can also help to identify specific character traits or parts of yourself you don't like when you notice them in others who are a part of your dreams. Especially if you are stuck in a particular situation in your life, recognizing other sides of yourself as projected in your dreams can help you draw on some new resources to deal with whatever you're struggling to overcome.

resonate at some level inside of you. Jung called this sensation a "click," a feeling of rightness. Be aware, however, that archetypes can play a creative or destructive role in dream work, depending on how you respond to them. As M. L. von Franz wrote in *Man and His Symbols*, archetypes are "creative when they inspire new ideas, destructive when these same ideas stiffen into conscious prejudices that inhibit further discoveries."

Building Associations

Once you begin working with your dreams, you'll become more attuned to yourself and to your environment. Even if you can't recall your dreams at first, or you remember them in bits and pieces, you might find yourself flashing on an image during the day. Sometimes a conversation or some event or situation might trigger your recall.

Through dreams, you can reassess situations from the past, revisit experiences, and gain new understanding. This is where free association comes in, because it taps into the wealth of experiences and memories your mind is storing. As you start to recall your dream symbols, try to associate them with something in your life. When you hit on something, associate that with something else, working your way back through your life until something "clicks." (Freud first popularized this method.)

For example, suppose the only thing you remember from a dream is that your significant other gave you a rose. What does a rose mean to you? Do you associate it with beauty? With thorns? With a sweet scent? Maybe you associate it with a garden. What does a garden mean to you? In this case, you would continue back through your memories until you hit something that felt right.

Amplification, the method that Jung advocated, is similar to association, but with one important difference. Instead of working backward through your past, with this technique you search for associations in the present. With the symbol of the rose, for instance, you would list everything that a rose means to you now.

⊛ Different Associations

Here's a quick way to distinguish between these two methods for dream association:

- Freud = Free Association = spontaneous, and it doesn't have to associate/connect to the dream
- Jung = Direct Association = also spontaneous, but it has to relate to the dream ▶

Creating Your Own Dream Dictionary

Dream symbols mean different things to different people. Unless you know what various objects mean to you, you won't have a clear idea about symbolic meanings in your dreams. To test this concept, consider the following list of common objects. Jot a word or phrase that defines this object next to the word. Don't refer to the contents of this dream dictionary. These are your personal interpretations. Without giving them much thought, note the first thing that comes to mind. If you can't think of anything, move on to the next word on the list.

airplane _____

airport _____

altar _____

balloon_____

basement _____

beach _____

boat _____

book_____

bridge _____

car _____

chair _____

children _____

church _____

classroom _____

computer _____

cross or crucifix _____

door _____

flowers _____

food _____

grass _____

gun _____

hallway _____

house _____

knife _____

lake _____

lamp _____

letters _____

mirror _____

money _____

moon _____

ocean _____

sidewalk _____

street_____

sun _____

table _____

telephone_____

television _____

theater _____

train _____

water _____

zoo _____

You can create additional entries in your personal dream dictionary by adding other common objects that appear in your dreams. You might also focus on specific types of symbols, for example, animals. To one person, a frog might represent luck; to another, the creature might represent transformation.

The problem with a static outlook on interpreting dreams is that the meanings of the symbols change as you change. What makes a seven-year-old happy probably doesn't thrill a twenty-one-year-old. Likewise, the joys or fears of a person at forty may be different from what pleases or concerns someone at seventy-five. So, periodically, update your personal dictionary—delete and add as necessary.

Dreams impart guidance even when you don't remember them. But once you have a fairly strong grasp of what certain symbols mean to you, you can become more than a passive observer in your dreams. You can request guidance from dreams—and receive answers!

Learning to Fly

Flying is probably one of the most common dream themes. If, however, you've never flown in your dreams, you can certainly learn how. People who fly regularly in their dreams report it as one of their most pleasurable dream activities. It's also quite valuable. Flying in your dreams can help

Comparing Your Dreams

Sharing and discussing your dreams with other family members and friends is an excellent way to gain insight. You might actually find similarities between your dream themes or scenarios and theirs, and this dialogue might lead you to a greater understanding of what the dreams mean. If you have not brought up the subject of dreams, try it. Suggest that you and a friend keep dream journals and compare them, or form a dream group that meets at specific times for discussions. The Internet is also an excellent way to share your dream experiences, and there are many Web sites dedicated to dream sharing.

you overcome the fear of flying in your waking life. It can release you from waking tensions, empower you, and completely revamp your ideas of what is possible.

In *The Dream Workbook*, Jill Morris offers an excellent method for learning to fly in your dreams. She suggests that before you go to sleep, you think about flying. Visualize what it would be like. As with any visualization, add as many details as you can—the feel of the wind through your hair, how the world would look from a vantage point fifty feet up, how your body would feel. Tell yourself you're going to fly in your dreams, repeat your intention out loud, and repeat it silently to yourself as you begin to drift off. If you wake up during the night, remind yourself of what you want to do.

If you don't succeed the first night, keep at it. Once you do begin to have flying dreams, you can attempt to increase their frequency by giving yourself a specific goal to accomplish in the dream.

Six Tips for Savvy Dream Analysis

As you begin to work with and assess your dreams, keep these basic, big-picture suggestions in mind.

- Watch for polarities in your dreams. These opposing symbols and metaphors often appear to help you measure and re-evaluate your thoughts and feelings about people, events, and situations. As author Layne Dalfen points out in *Dreams Do Come True*, "If you are underreacting to a given situation, the opposite over-reaction will often appear in the dream."
- Pay attention to what is missing in your dreams just as much as what is there. For instance, if you dream you are in danger, hurt, or in need of assistance, consider whether anyone is there in your dream to help. A dream of this sort might have more to do with feelings about having to deal with things on your own, than with the specific danger itself.
- Be aware of the patterns in your waking life. Often, these same roles, parts, and themes play out in our dreams—just in ways that are more complicated, hidden, or harder to deconstruct.

continued on following page

Sometimes in a flying dream, you won't be able to sustain height or even the flight itself. But if you have confidence in yourself and you aren't afraid, you'll make more and more progress with flying dreams. Once you find that flight is possible in a dream, play around with your techniques; be innovative, and try different types of flight.

continued from previous page

You'll be better equipped to deal with what your dream patterns mean if you are aware of the patterns in your life, the roles you play, and what your relationships with others represent. Then you can forge a closer connection between your waking and sleeping life.

- Watch for broad themes, but also don't overlook obscure details in your dreams. Focusing on the dominant images can sometimes obscure or cause you to gloss over the things that don't jump out at you immediately. Remember, it's not only the main themes that mean the most when it comes to dreams.

- Never judge your dreams. Just because something that makes you uncomfortable happens in your dreams, that doesn't mean it will play out in real life. Dreams simply provide you with a safe place to explore feelings and emotions, and to practice dealing with new, unexpected, or strange situations.

- Consider your dream symbols on more than one level. Often, there can be layers of metaphors in your dreams, and the symbols can represent different things when examined in different ways.

Dreaming of Good Health

There are many different, common symbols that are generally indicative of good health. These include the sun; clear, cool water; a flourishing garden; brilliant stars; the colors gold, green, and pink; a God image; an angel; or a healer. Use these to brainstorm and come up with more symbols of your own. You might want to create a section in your dream journal where you can list symbols of good health that arise from your dreams.

If you're an avid swimmer, for instance, you might find that in your dreams, the various moods and color of the ocean or a swimming pool depict states of your health. Likewise, if you enjoy gardening, the state of your dream garden might also tell you a great deal about your health. If you love horses, then a dream image of a robust, exuberant horse could represent a healthy image of your body. Be innovative in your associations; let your imagination run wild. (Healing dreams and their incubation will be discussed in greater detail in Chapter 5.)

Other Prevalent Themes

There are also certain other dream themes that seem to be common to many of us. The themes probably don't qualify as archetypal; that is, they are not forces within us. Rather, their genesis usually lies in our daily lives and experiences. Sometimes, they express fears or anxieties; other times, they express joy or triumph. In all cases, though, they speak volumes about the things that are on our minds and in our hearts, so they deserve attention.

These common themes often creep into recurring dreams, and when they do, it might be an indication that you're stuck in a particular pattern or that some issue in your life has yet to be resolved. Some of the most common themes include the following, which will be covered in detail in this dictionary:

- Falling
- Taking an examination for which you're unprepared
- Attending a class
- Being naked
- Losing keys, a wallet, a purse, or a briefcase
- Riding a bus, train, or plane

- Having your teeth fall out
- Finding money

This is by no means a definitive list. Themes, like societies themselves, undoubtedly change over time. For the children of today, new themes, such as UFOs and/or alien abductions, computer system crashes, extreme weather, airplane disasters, or other popular media topics might be prevalent.

Chapter 5

Common Dream Types

Although each person's individual experience with dreams is different, there are certain types of dreams and themes that are common. As you continue to work at remembering your dreams, you will begin to recognize the various types. Once you learn how to identify some of these broad dream categories, you will be able to build a context for your dreams, and this framework will help you to gain insight into their meanings. Pay close attention to those sorts of dreams that resonate for you, and use this information to help you explore your own specific dream scenarios further.

Following are the more common categories of dream types:

- **Everyday Dreaming,** which will be explained in the following section, is the most common type of dreaming. These are the sorts of dreams that are often triggered when your unconscious brain plays on the events and situations of the day.

- **Desire Dreaming** is characterized by situations in which your unconscious mind explores situations you either would like to happen or, in contrast, situations that you would be quite troubled by were they ever to occur.

- **Recurrent Dreaming** happens when you have similar dreams again and again.

- **Fear or Anxiety Dreaming** is quite common. These dreams can range from vividly true-to-life to absurdly unrealistic.

- **Nightmare Dreaming** falls into a subset of the fear/anxiety category. Because they are so common—and so terrifying—a separate examination is in order.

Everyday Dreams

Everyday dreams are normal dreams—but what's "normal," anyway? Let's say you recently had a dream about your mailman. At first glance, this dream doesn't seem "normal" at all. When you're awake, you rarely think of this guy, yet suddenly there he is at the center of your dream world, fighting and defeating a bunch of three-eyed, brain-sucking trolls that are after you—and conquering your heart as well!

This is what we call a "test" dream. It's an everyday dream, because it's simply you, your unconscious, testing out the things you would never even consider doing in real life. Does this mean you should go out on a date with your mailman? Well, not unless you're single and you really want to.

The point is, this dream—as strange as it might be—does not necessarily have to contain a lot of higher meaning. It's simply letting you test out possibilities. Here are other examples of everyday dreams:

- You watch an old episode of *Buffy the Vampire Slayer* on TV, and then you have a dream in which you yourself are slaying monsters and vampires. (Another version: You and your friend turn into the monsters and vampires!)
- You meet someone who reminds you of an acquaintance you haven't thought about in years, and then you have a dream about that old acquaintance.

- You're on a diet, trying to lose weight, and you have a dream about food.
- You've been thinking about going on vacation and later dream about surfing in Hawaii or hiding out from the KGB in communist Russia.
- Someone is getting on your nerves at work and you have a dream that you're a gladiator in the Coliseum in ancient Rome—and your colleague is your opponent!

Everyday dreams may have symbols, but you also have to take into consideration the overall general theme of the dream to determine what it is that your unconscious is trying to sort out. Chances are, if the dream is based on everyday happenings—even if it takes on a surreal, unnatural setting—you can rest assured that your unconscious mind is simply exploring those happenings and their implications in your life.

Dreams of Desire

Dreams of desire involve wish fulfillment (or wish negation). In other words, your unconscious creates a scene in which you get what you want and live happily ever after, or you get the opposite of what you want and you don't live happily ever after.

If, for example, you have a dream that your significant other is cheating on you, does it mean that it's really true? Or that it's going to happen? Probably not, because this is another "what if" dream—you are testing the limits of reality. If you are single and have a dream of meeting your perfect mate and bringing her home to meet your family, is it really going to happen? Is this sort of dream a prophecy? Probably not. Again, this is a wish dream. Keep in mind that wish/desire dreams can be positive or negative.

Here are additional examples of desire dreams:

- You're stranded on a desert island with a friend, and when your friend finds and then jumps into the only lifeboat there is, he or she leaves you behind.
- You're at a big movie premiere with a famous star, and everyone's taking your picture.
- You're in a bathing suit at a beach party and everyone is complimenting you on what a great body you have.
- Your friends are talking about you and

you're invisible to them, listening to what they're saying.

- In real life, you're vehemently against the killing of animals, but in a dream, you're wearing fur or you are out in the woods hunting.

Recurring Dreams

Recurring dreams—when you have the same dream or minor variations on the same dream over and over—signal that you're stuck in or on something, whether it be a situation, relationship, feeling, action, or anything else. If the same things keep happening again and again in your dreams, this points to a need to change something that is persisting in some area of yourself or your life. Pay attention, therefore, to recurring situations in your waking life, whether in terms of something you need to stop happening, or something you need to occur in your life that isn't taking place.

A dream series is a different subset of this phenomenon. According to Layne Dalfen in *Dreams Do Come True,* a dream series "is a collection of dreams often over a short period of time, where there are recurring metaphors, symbols, or themes." In these instances, the situations or details of the dreams might change or be more significantly different than in typical recurring dreams. If you pay attention to these details and keep track of them, eventually, in spite of the similarities, you'll notice the differences more and more. Those realizations will give you clues to the meanings or solutions to the problems about which you're dreaming.

In the case of repetitive dreams, Dalfen says, no change is shown and, therefore, "no progress, no movement on the subject" occurs. In other words, you don't resolve a problem situation through repetitive dreams. "Progressive dreams, on the other hand, show movement," she writes. Be mindful of any sort of changes in repetitive dreams—change in the context of the symbols and images of the dream, but also any change in your feelings or actions within the dreams. Notice if you're responding differently. This awareness will help you to chart the progress you make through your dreams.

Finally, if you recall multiple dreams in the same night, look for connections because even dreams that seem very dissimilar on the surface can be linked by similar themes that form a more subtle dream series.

Fear or Anxiety Dreams

Dreams that elicit fear and anxiety are fairly common. Fear dreams can run the gamut from a Mafia don with a pistol chasing you down a dark alley, to a giant spider attacking you. The commonality is that there's always an element of fear that relates back to what you identify with as frightening in your dream—whether you have a fear of monsters, spiders, or even your boss. Most of the time, these fears are irrational and don't pose a true threat in real life. After all, what are the chances of a jumbo arachnid finding its way into your bedroom at night? But that's of no consequence—it's terrifying nevertheless.

A fear or anxiety dream is actually a test dream taken to the next level. These dreams usually relate to fears or issues you've pushed aside or tried to ignore. Monsters and supernatural dangers in fear and anxiety dreams are often symbolic of real-life fears. Or it might be your subconscious's way of testing how much you can handle. What on earth *would* you do if demons really wandered around in your backyard? Dreams such as these can show you how you would react under extreme pressure.

Sometimes, the actual symbols themselves are not as important as what the overall theme of the dream is trying to tell you. For example, you know that the chances of your getting into an elevator and having it bounce out of the building, skyrocket to the heavens, and then drop five thousand stories with you in it, is not something that's about to happen any time soon. Yet, it's perfectly possible that you might have a dream about it. Perhaps in this dream you are trying to deal with your fear of losing control. The symbolism is in the entire dream, and the particular symbol is just the embodiment or reflection of that. Any sort of "out of control" dream, like the above example, has to do with the fear you have of something happening in your life that you can't get a grip on.

Nightmares: Where They Come From, What They Mean

Nightmares are the most extreme versions of fear and anxiety dreams. Whereas the fear of being unprepared for a test—even when you've been out of school for years—might still leave you feeling anxious and nervous, nightmares often leave you trembling with terror. Ask any three-year-old about his or her nightmares, and he or she will probably tell you about dreams of being pursued by horrible animals—grinning monkeys, fire-breathing dragons, ferocious wolves, or dangerous lions.

Quite often, children's nightmares occur after a scolding or punishment by parents. They also occur when a child is ill or in transition, for example, during a divorce or a move from one home to another. Sometimes they seem to happen for no apparent external reason. But if you gently interview children about their nightmares, you can usually get to the source of what caused them.

As children near the age of six, their nightmares change. Instead of pursuit and threats by animals, the scary encounters they dream of might be with a bully in the class or down the street. These nightmares often deal with anxieties and fears in children's waking lives. This pattern can also be true of adults, although once you're grown, nightmares become somewhat more complicated.

In *The Bedside Guide to Dreams*, Stase Michaels outlines three different kinds of nightmares that are common to adults. "In the first kind, you face your actual fears. In the second, you deal with the pain and trauma in yourself and in your life. The third kind is the most common type of dream and is reflected in the saying 'I have met the enemy, and it is I." In other words, in this last type of nightmare, you encounter a part of yourself that you would rather not see. The person or event you're reacting to in your dream hits an all-too-familiar chord because it reflects some element in yourself that you would rather keep hidden.

Nightmares often are the mirror to the parts of yourself that keep popping up on you, no matter how hard you try to keep them down. The same holds true, for that matter, in all sorts of dreams, and a variety of situations, people, and even inanimate objects can embody these things. Dream symbols don't necessarily need to be scary to illuminate the less-than-perfect sides of ourselves that we'd prefer not to see. As Layne Dalfen explains in *Dreams Do Come True,* "We project these [disowned, alienated] character traits because it helps us remain disconnected from them. We're trying to deny we have these parts that we don't want." Carl Jung called these uncomfortable parts of yourself your Shadow—the unexamined aspects of your personality that need to be developed.

Confronting Your Fears

If you are often plagued by nightmares, the most important thing to do is confront your fears.

As Ernest Hartman, a psychoanalyst and author of *The Nightmare*, says, when it comes to night terrors—the terrifying dreams that cause you to wake up screaming in a total, disoriented panic—"There is sometimes a sense that these people are unable or unwilling to notice or express strong feelings in the day time; in them, the night terror episodes may express a kind of outbreak of repressed emotions."

Analyzing Your Nightmares

If you suffer from recurring nightmares, try analyzing one of the themes. Consider the prevalent images, the spot where the dream takes place, and how you act and react. Are there any puns or metaphors you can pick up on that might hold clues to the meaning of the dream? How does the dream end? If you've never confronted your fear in this nightmare, rewrite the ending so you do. ◗

Most people don't obsess about the things or situations they fear. They simply react when confronted with the fear. Confronting your fears and emotions will help you to seize control of frightening situations in your dreams, and it will also help you to work out your anxieties—most likely the root cause of the nightmares—in waking life.

By consciously recognizing what you fear, you take the first step to overcoming it.

Also, pay attention to your strengths in a nightmare. Often, we get so caught up in the fear we feel that we neglect to consider our own responses in a nightmare. If, for instance, you have a nightmare that you are being pursued by some sort of menacing attacker, and yet you escape in your dream, think about what this says regarding your own resiliency and your ability to come through under pressure, in the midst of a trying situation.

Nightmares, although upsetting, do have their benefits. Sometimes, if they are startling enough, they can actually help you to make changes and create movement in your life. Remember, nightmares wake you up with a frightful start because that's exactly what they are meant to do—give you a wakeup call.

Warning Nightmares

Sometimes, nightmares seem to be a literal warning about something—your health, your car, a pending accident, or a neighborhood to avoid. But before you jump to any conclusions about your nightmare being a literal warning, exhaust the other possibilities.

Look for metaphors. Scrutinize the dream for hints that it illuminates some part of your personality you don't want to know about. Be honest. Does it depict one of your actual fears? Does it address a rejected part of yourself?

You should only consider the nightmare as a true warning once you determine that it doesn't fall into any of these other categories.

- **Vividness:** Warning dreams are usually very vivid.
- **Your reactions:** If a dream is a warning, you'll most likely react in the same ways you would react in waking life in a similar situation or event.
- **Duplication of details:** In a warning dream, your house looks like the actual house you live in. Your mother looks like your real mother. There is a literal feel to the dream that is lacking in other dreams.

Helping Children to Cope with Nightmares

As discussed, nightmares can stem from un-resolved or fearsome situations in waking life, and a good way to help children work through a nightmare is to help them connect with some sense of Universal Protection. At an early age, that might mean feeling a sense that something is with them, such as an angel that watches over and protects them from harm. Let them tell you what is best for them, and then you can reinforce that source of security.

If a deceased relative or friend visits a child in a dream, that person might be there to provide comfort when it is needed or to warn of potential problems. If children grow to be comfortable and trust their dreams, they can learn to be less upset about these types of startling dreams and instead incorporate the deceased relative or friend as part of their guidance system. In this way, children will learn to believe that the messages in their dreams need not be menacing or frightening; instead, they can be for the good if they use the information positively.

Chapter 6

More Advanced Dream Types

In addition to the common dream types you've just learned about, this chapter will explore some additional dream categories that might seem more challenging or unusual to you. Some of these, such as lucid dreaming, are acquired techniques, and in time, as you become more skilled in your dream work, you might want to practice them. Other types, such as telepathic or prophetic dreaming, are less common in occurrence and cannot be controlled in the same way. But even if you never experience them, it's worth familiarizing yourself with what they are about, simply to broaden your understanding of dream work's scope.

This chapter is simply meant to serve as an introduction to these techniques. In order to understand them fully, however, more in-depth research is necessary. If any of the more mysterious, complicated, or advanced dream categories intrigue you, you might consider doing additional reading, as suggested in the reference appendix of this book.

• **Lucid Dreaming,** which will be discussed in the next section, is a dream situation where the dreamer is aware of being in a dream state and is able to interact with the situation.

• **Ritualistic Dreaming,** which can be linked to lucid dreaming, occurs when an individual purposefully tries to create an atmosphere conducive to receiving spiritually centered dreams.

• **Programmed Dreaming,** also related to lucid dreaming, happens when a person tries to dream of specific imagery by using presleep emblems or symbolism.

• **Spiritually Generated Dreaming,** discussed further in this chapter, is less common but of particular import; these sorts of dreams involve a deeper spiritual meaning or significance.

• **Healing Dreaming,** which will also be explored in this chapter, occurs when messages that provide insight into a medical treatment, physical condition, or even an emotional or spiritual wound filter in through your unconscious.

• **Past-Life Dreaming** is believed to reveal a previous incarnation of the dreamer's soul.

• **Telepathic Dreaming,** discussed in general later in this chapter, involves communication between your mind and that of another without personal contact.

• **Prophetic Dreaming,** examined briefly in this chapter, is precognitive and depicts events that will occur in the future.

• **Symbolic Dreaming,** sometimes related to prophetic dreaming, involves representational dream themes containing a broader meaning that is sometimes hard to decipher.

Lucid Dreams

A lucid dream is one in which you're aware that you're dreaming. It might begin as a normal dream, but at some point you "wake up" inside the dream. Then, depending on your skill, you can manipulate the action in the dream, to mold it—to create it second by second.

For years, lucid dreaming was primarily the domain of parapsychologists, a critical factor in discouraging mainstream scientists from studying it. But in recent years, there has been an explosive interest in lucid dreaming. Stephen LaBerge, a pioneer of lucid dreaming research, attributes this surge of interest, in part, to several landmark books written in the 1960s and 1970s, including *Lucid Dreams*, by English parapsychologist Celia Green; *The Dream Game* by Ann Faraday; and *Creative Dreaming* by Patricia Garfield. Even though serious scientific research of lucid dreaming didn't take place until the 1970s, it has been recognized for centuries, particularly by Tibetan yoga masters.

Frequently, lucid dreams are first experienced "accidentally." In other words, no special preparations are made, but a dream suddenly turns lucid. Basically, you realize you are awake and still dreaming. If you're lucky, the experience will last more than a few seconds.

For some, lucidity might arise for the first time from a nightmare. But for most dreamers, LaBerge says, lucidity happens when you recognize some glaring inconsistency or bizarre factor in your dream. Other times, a first-time experience is triggered when you realize your dream is very familiar, that you've dreamed it before. LaBerge calls this entry into a lucid dream *deja reve*.

One way of determining whether or not you're having a lucid dream is, quite simply, by doing a reality check. "Reality testing" is a reasoning process normally delegated to the waking brain, but it is also one of the elements that distinguishes lucid dreams from other kinds of dreams. With practice, you won't even have to ask if you're dreaming. Once you recognize some anomaly or bizarre event in the dream, your realization will be instantaneous.

Inducing Lucid Dreams

If you have never awakened inside a dream and would like to sample the experience, or if you've spontaneously entered a lucid dream in the past and would like to explore this region of dreaming further, there are methods you can try to induce lucidity. The best time to enter a lucid dream is either just as you fall asleep or as you awaken after a night's sleep. If you fall asleep easily and quickly, with practice you can enter a lucid dream within minutes of lying down. LaBerge suggests using a counting method, such as suggesting to yourself, "One, I'm dreaming; two, I'm dreaming . . ." and so on. Eventually, at some point, you will, in fact, be dreaming.

Alternately, as you are falling asleep, you can also focus on one particular thing—a visualization, your breath or heartbeat, how your body feels, or whatever you choose. "If you keep the mind sufficiently active while the tendency to enter REM sleep is strong," writes LaBerge, "you feel your body fall asleep but you, that is to say, your consciousness, remains awake."

🌞 The Power of Visualization

Presleep visualization plays an important role in preparing you for a journey through programmed dreaming. If attempting these sorts of techniques, it might help to use symbols and imagery that you feel will inspire a spiritual dream. For example, since the eye is regarded as the window to the soul and represents "vision" on all levels of being, envisioning an eye can be one option that provides a defined cue to your subconscious and superconscious mind. ❱

Or, you might find that a lucid state is easier to obtain after you've slept awhile. Since your longest period of REM sleep is toward morning, try not to open your eyes when you wake. Lie quietly and let your dream images surround and flow through you. Then turn over on your side or change positions. The act of moving may allow you to think of yourself as awake as well as dreaming.

The Benefits of Lucid Dreaming

No matter what method you use to reach the world of lucid dreams, once you begin your journey, the benefits are enormous. The dreamer who is aware of being in a dream state has the power to interact with the images, even change them for a more positive outcome. This awareness is particularly empowering for nightmares, which embody and personify our fears and pains. By engaging the misgivings and fears head-on and changing the outcome of the dream, you'll realize that you also have the power to transform waking reality.

To illustrate the power of lucid dreaming, an example might be in order. Say you are especially preoccupied with your work projects, the problems you might be having with them, or the things that might be going wrong. Perhaps you feel that your energies aren't being directed effectively and you're spinning your wheels. In a lucid dream, you have the power to change that situation by deliberately directing those issues differently. You might even dream of how you can transform your reality. If you are able to accomplish different outcomes in your dreams, this will reinforce the belief that you can direct your energies toward a better outcome in real life as well.

Whatever your concerns might be, here are some of the general benefits of lucid dreaming:

- You can overcome your fears by directly confronting them in your lucid dreams.
- You can increase your self-knowledge, which expands your awareness.
- By consciously facing danger in your dreams, you develop self-confidence, which spills into your everyday life.
- You can solve problems in the dream state that will benefit your waking life.

Keep in mind that your intention to explore the world of lucid dreaming is vital in triggering such a dream.

Spiritually Generated Dreams

As you've learned in the last chapter, most dreams you experience have to do with odd things your mind retains during the day or week, or other concerns you've been mulling over. Occasionally, however, some people experience dreams that have deeper spiritual meaning or significance. These dreams are in the minority, however, so don't be disappointed if the work you do with your dreams does not produce these sorts of results.

How can you know for certain if you have had a dream of import—a dream in which a Spirit or the higher self has visited you? There are several signs to watch for:

- The dream produces a dramatic emotional response (fear, joy, sadness, release, and so on).
- The dream exhibits uncanny realism that leaves the dreamer somewhat confused upon waking.
- The dream repeats for several nights in a row (three being a common number).
- The dream includes information or learning to which the dreamer has no conscious access.
- Images from the dream disrupt waking reality by returning to the forefront of the dreamer's thoughts regularly throughout the next few days.
- The dream includes a blazing light or

sense of a higher power, which is often overwhelming to the dreamer.

- The dream is unusually multisensual. For example, if you do not usually have a sense of smell in your dreams, this additional dimension points to a uniquely multifaceted experience.

Healing Dreams

Healing dreams are not as common as some other types of dreams, but they can occur when they are needed. Healing dreams might originate from either the unconscious or Universal Mind. Sometimes, when you are too consciously involved with your own medical condition or the condition of loved ones, it's difficult to look at the situation rationally. In these instances, you might not be hearing what you are unconsciously telling yourself.

Dreams are a good way for your unconscious mind to get that message up to your conscious mind, and valuable clues to your medical condition, and possibly even your treatment, can come from your unconscious mind. The same might hold true for information given to you about others, including friends and family.

Your dreams can provide you with a different perspective.

A healing dream does not necessarily have to be related to a physical ailment. This type of dream can also help in resolving old emotional or relational conflicts that have affected people's lives. They might include new insights that will help you resolve, either in your own mind or in communication with others, a situation that needs to be healed. In fact, these types of dream images sometimes come to you with information that helps you figure out how to say or write the appropriate words to someone. A healing dream might even come in the form of inspiration to compose or create a work of art or a poem that will bring about this sort of healing.

If you think you might be having dreams related to healing, think about how you receive the information. Does it come to you in symbols, actual pictures, voices, feelings, or in some other way? Do you wake up with a feeling of knowing that healing is occurring, or does your dream leave you with a picture image that demonstrates this?

Before you go to sleep, you might want to try asking that your dreams send you healing information for you or others. If you get answers, keep track of what they are and how often they come through. If you receive bits of healing poems, music, or artistic ideas in your dreams, consider how you can flesh out these snippets in your waking life, in order to craft something that will help to heal yourself and/or others.

Dream Incubation for Good Health

The first step in using your dreams for healing is to accept that it's possible to induce a dream—any dream.

Before actually attempting to induce a healing dream, find a quiet spot where you won't be interrupted—a shady spot in your yard, a secluded place on a beach, your own bedroom, or any other place where you can focus without being distracted.

As you settle down, begin by relaxing your body. One good way to do this is to relax your muscles consciously, from your head to your toes, and feel the tension drain out through the soles of your feet. Or you can simply focus on the warmth of the sunlight or the scent of the air.

Once you're fully relaxed, you're ready for the next step. Have a clear idea of the dream you want to induce and concentrate on it. You can enhance your concentration by repeating a word or phrase that has something to do with that dream. If you choose a phrase, just be careful of how you word it, and keep it positive. Instead of saying that your tumor is gone, for example, it would be better to say: "I am healed."

🌀 The Power of Your Belief

In *Creative Dreaming*, author Patricia Garfield points out another way to induce a dream, and that's to "visualize the desired dream as though it is happening." This is no different, really, than consciously visualizing something you want to happen in waking life. Belief is paramount— belief that it will happen; that it's possible; that your mind, your being, is wise and capable. Believe, intend, imagine, and charge the visualization with emotions. Also, keep the visualization in the present rather than in some dim future. ❭

If the healing dream doesn't come to you the first time you try it, keep at it. Share the process with someone you trust—a spouse, sibling, parent, friend, son, or daughter. By sharing, you make it even more real. Read about dreams and other people's experiences with healing.

When Louise Hay, author of *You Can Heal Your Life*, was diagnosed with cancer, her physician wanted to perform a hysterectomy as soon as possible. But Hay resisted. She told him she wanted some time to work on the problem herself.

She completely revamped the externals in her life—nutrition, exercise, and work schedule. Then she began to work with her beliefs through visualization, affirmations, and prayer. She created mental stages on which she spoke to the various people in her past who had hurt her deeply and she saw herself forgiving them. She also experienced self-forgiveness by learning to love herself.

Within six months, her cancer was in remission.

The bottom line is that the inner is a reflection of the outer. As such, your dreams reflect what's going on in your body; your body reflects the texture of your dreams.

But don't wait until you're sick to reinforce your health. As Patricia Garfield notes in *Creative Dreaming*, "You can suggest to yourself dream images believed to be reflective of good health and thereby encourage well-being in yourself."

Past-Life Dreams

One type of dream that often starts in childhood and may or may not continue into adulthood deals with a past life. Children may not recognize that what they are dreaming is from a past life, but they may notice that in their dream, they and their family members appear in different roles. Proceed with caution when exploring these types of dreams; professional therapists and other experts spend years investigating these sorts of phenomenon, and still there are no definitive answers. For your purposes in this book, simply take these scenarios into consideration, and then if you are interested, you can pursue other sources of information on the topic.

One way that people recognize or identify a past-life dream is by noticing if it is set during a different time period. These types of dreams might also be repetitious because, according to some who have studied these types of dreams, it might involve a theme that was imprinted in the soul of the past life. It's not unusual for the past-life dream to be traumatic—many of these dreams are nightmares. For example, a past-life dream may be an event that led up to a death scene, with the dream ending before the actual event. Upon waking, a feeling of terror often lingers.

Often, these dreams have visual images that can be recognized. In some instances, the dream location might seem familiar and yet as though it doesn't belong to your lifetime. Sometimes that distinction is easy to make, and sometimes it is not. A child might not recognize the difference of a few years, whereas an adult would. Also, if the turnaround time between incarnations is short, the child might blend his or her current life with the one that he or she experiences just previously.

🔆 Sharing Past-Life Dreams

Past-life dreams can be shared, often by members of the same family. These dreams can go unnoted for years, unless someone brings up the subject for discussion. One couple, for example, found they both had the same recurring dream of drowning, and they eventually discovered that their son had been having the same dream. ▶

One way to gain insight into these possibilities is to mine the various details of the dream for clues regarding the specifics of the past-life scenario. If there are people in the dream, for instance, it's important to note how they are dressed. Are they wearing modern clothes, or do their clothes appear to date from a particular time period? Sometimes, the dreamer can see themselves in the dream, and other times they are only experiencing the action as it happens, as if they were watching a movie. In these instances, hypnosis sometimes helps to uncover more information about who the characters in the dream might have been and what the situations mean.

Dreams and the ESP Connection

Dreams are a great medium for receiving psychic information. They come at a time when your conscious mind is at rest and open to the messages of your unconscious and your Universal Mind. Because your conscious mind is so active, perhaps you might not relax enough while you are awake to receive the information that is there for you. At night, you might have many dreams, but most of them go unnoticed. Even if you are aware of having dreamt when you wake up, you might quickly forget the contents of those dreams.

Extrasensory perception (ESP) dreams are often telepathic (involving mind-to-mind communication) or precognitive (involving events in the future). These types of dreams might pertain to you directly, or to your family, friends or acquaintances, strangers or public figures, and private or public events and situations. They are as diverse as the people who dream them.

These types of dreams might be extraordinarily vivid and incredibly colorful, with intense emotional content. Ordinary dreams can also possess these qualities, of course, but with an ESP dream there are distinctive characteristics that stick with you.

Many ESP dreams involve the people who are closest to you, but in the dreams your relationship to the people might be completely different from what they are in waking life. In his book *Parent-Child Telepathy*, psychiatrist Berthold Schwartz recorded over five hundred instances of telepathy within his own family. Many of the episodes involved trivial but fascinating incidents from daily life, which led Schwartz to believe that telepathy is the "missing link" in communication between parents and their children.

Psychiatrist Montague Ullman notes that in his research during the 1960s and 1970s telepathic dreams were more frequently reported by women than by men. However, given the increased public awareness about the value of dreams, this division might no longer be true.

While ESP dream research was once confined to dream laboratories and conducted by scientists, it has spread into dream groups, where participants may be bound together only by their interest in dreams. In many of these groups, no professional dream researchers are involved. Dream experiments in telepathy have even been conducted among strangers communicating through online services.

In the course of a lifetime, you might recall a single telepathic or precognitive dream or you may recall hundreds. It depends on how actively you explore your personal dreamscapes and how deeply you penetrate the layers of yourself.

As you become more proficient at interpreting your dreams, telepathic and precognitive dreams will be easier to spot. You might want to keep these kinds of dreams in a special section in your journal or mark them in some way. These dreams are your most intimate link to your own future.

Prophetic Dreams

Many of the great prophets throughout history have relied on their dreams to provide the insights that helped rulers make their decisions about the future. These predictions included floods, famines, and other weather changes. They also included predictions of wars and threats to the people, the land, and even to the rulers themselves.

Although a subset of ESP dreams, prophetic dreams are extremely complex and require a separate discussion. Here, we're getting into difficult territory. Prophecy dreams sometimes have a mix of all the other dream categories, so they're hard to pinpoint. Usually, though, if you've had a prophecy dream, you know it. If you're not sure, you probably didn't have one. Prophecy dreams can involve receiving advice from a strange or unknown source or seeing a situation before it happens; they also typically contain strong symbolism, which you can somehow interpret.

Advice from a Strange or Unknown Source

Let's say you have a dream in which your dog talks to you and gives you advice. This can be an everyday dream or a prophecy dream. How can you tell the difference? Well, if the source of this knowledge comes from you, from your unconscious, it's an everyday dream: You're using the dog in your dream as a way for you to talk to yourself. But, on the other hand, if you have no idea where the things your dog says came from, chances are you're receiving a gift, words coming from a higher spiritual level.

⚙️ Simultaneous Dreaming

A dream experienced simultaneously between two or more people is known as a shared dream. Some shared dreams are also prophetic, and they signal a world event to come. These dreams may happen within a short time span, often only a few days before the event actually happens. Other shared dreams are simpler—they might involve something that you share with a friend, and then later, both of you realize that you had a similar dream about that discussion. ▶

Here's another example: In your dream, a woman walks up to you in the street and tells you that if you don't stop eating hamburgers, you're going to have health problems and pass out in a Laundromat. Is this a prophecy dream? No, this is your unconscious warning you of things you're already probably well aware of but, perhaps, have chosen to ignore.

On the other hand, let's say that you have a dream about a queen who tells you to take her hand, and you have no idea what it means, either in the dream or in waking life. This is probably prophetic advice. At some point in the near future, you'll be in a situation in which you'll have to use this information. It's up to you to figure out when. It could happen when you're in a meeting at work or when you're strolling down the street with your significant other. In any case, you'll actually feel the two realities come together. The moment will have a kind of slow-motion effect and you'll sense that this is where your dream world meets the real world. That's how you'll know.

Seeing a Situation Before It Happens

Remember, prophetic dreams aren't the sort that happen all the time. If, however, you are prone to receiving messages in your dreams regarding things or events to come, consider whether there is some sort of pattern to them. Prophetic dreams can predict simple, everyday things that actually happen, such as meeting an old friend on the street, or predicting the questions that will be on a test before it's taken. They can also foretell of events that might take place on a worldwide scale. Some people dream of disasters before they happen, such as plane crashes, assassinations of famous people, or even wars.

Many times, what seems like a dream that will come true in reality is actually a testing dream. There is a problem with assuming that a testing dream is a prophecy dream. Just think about the concept of a self-fulfilling prophecy: If you believe something will happen, you very well might start a chain of events that will actually lead to its occurrence.

So, for example, if you have a dream in which you and your sister have a big fight and then she storms out the house, angry, and has a car accident, what does this mean? Does it mean that she's going to have a car accident? Should you be extra nice to her so that you two don't quarrel? Well, yes, be nice to her, by all means. You can even warn her to drive safely, as well. But chances are, this is not a prophecy dream. It's an everyday dream that tests your fears.

High Intensity

Most prophecy dreams involve more intense symbolism than the above example. Consequently, when you have one, you will recognize it as such. Remember that when it comes to dreams, symbols cannot be translated into a universal language. This is because your unconscious is doing the interpreting. Each one of us is a separate, unique entity with different built-in features and filters that affect how we see the world. Therefore, even if a higher force is passing on a prophetic message to you, your dream will simply give you a picture in accordance with that which your unconscious finds comfortable or familiar. And this is what makes the dream easier for you to digest, absorb, and understand. So, while a dream book of universal signs such as this might be helpful, the symbols in your dream will not necessarily mean the same things for you that they do for others. Use your own judgment when working with these dream symbols and use them as a stepping stone to other, more personal associations as you see fit.

Here is an example: One woman has a prophetic dream that only occurs when a member of her family is about to pass over. Instead of the family member coming into her dream to visit her (a common happening in prophecy dreams of this sort), she dreams of water. And while this may seem strange to most people, this woman knows that when she has this kind of "water" dream, it is an indication that someone she knows is about to pass away.

Water, as a universal symbol, usually means prosperity, happiness, and rebirth, so it's odd that this woman would dream of water when the theme of her prophecy dream deals with a relative passing away. The point is, each person's symbolism is different, and you should construct your own dream glossary. This is essential in order to interpret not just prophetic dreams, but other sorts of dreams as well.

Symbolic Dreams

Once in a while, you might experience a dream that feels like a riddle. It could involve snippets and pieces of events in your life, usually close in time to when the dream is experienced. These snippets might be from news accounts, or they might be drawn from some memory in your unconscious mind. These pieces are woven into the dream theme but are not in keeping with the actual events.

Symbolic dreams can occur in sequences or segments, and they might be experienced over the course of several different nights or weeks. Like prophetic dreams in general, these dreams can relate to you specifically, or to events that are taking place in the world. Dream themes can address events that have already taken place, or with events that have yet to happen.

Symbolic dreams are easily dismissed as non-sense dreams. These are dreams that are often attributed to too much rich food or experiences you might have lived through earlier in the day. Even when a dream seems to make no sense, however, make a note of it in your dream journal. Over time, as is the case with all dreams, you might find a pattern developing in your symbolic dreams that will lead you to the right interpretation.

Symbolic Interpretation

To help you to identify a dream that has symbolic content, note the apparent theme of the dream. Is it repeated in the dream? Do you have the same dream or a series of different dreams with the same recurring theme? Think about the specifics: Are there people, animals, or other beings in your symbolic dreams? Are there houses or rooms of a house? Consider how these dreams make you feel, and whether you can make sensory connections. Can you hear voices or other sounds, for instance? Do the actions in the dreams make any sense to you at first review? Take time to examine all of the components of these dreams, to help you decipher those things that might be of symbolic import.

Part Two

Dream Dictionary

abdomen: Seeing your abdomen in a dream suggests the gestation or digestion of a new idea or phase of your life. If your abdomen is swollen, the birth of a new project might be imminent.

abyss: In the tarot, this is the place where faith is tested, the place from which the Fool leaps to discover his or her magick. No surprise, then, that this dream can represent obstacles, uncertainty, and also fear—of the unknown, of failure, of your own capabilities, or whatever else is pressing on your mind. After all, the image of teetering over the edge of cliff, chasm, precipice, or pit—images that are all related to abysses—is one that is keenly chiseled into our collective consciousness. These notions all relate back to the fear of falling into a dangerous unknown or a depth of emptiness.

In a totally different sense, an abyss may represent fertility (the womb), and new beginnings. (See also *chasm, cliff, pit,* and *precipice.*)

actor or actress: Perhaps you're only seeing your own or someone else's persona, the side that is shown to the world. Seeing yourself as an actor in the spotlight suggests a desire for publicity or a more public life. A dream of this type can also imply that you're acting out a role or "putting on an act" for someone else.

Adam and Eve: If you dream of the biblical couple who lived in the traditional Paradise, it means that some event will rob you of success. Remember, Adam and Eve weren't exactly models of success: They were banished from Paradise. Therefore, this dream is telling you to beware, and to tread softly. If you dream of Adam in a fig leaf and Eve with only a serpent covering her waist and abdomen, treachery and evil will quell your fortune.

afternoon: Dreams that take place in the afternoon suggest clarity and lengthiness of duration. If you dream you are with friends in the afternoon, then positive and lasting associations might soon be formed.

agate: Eye agate, traditionally used for protection from the evil eye, represents the need for safety.

age: Dreaming of someone in various stages of life can imply different things. Often, for example, we associate babies with newness, freshness, and innocence. Dreams of children might bring you back to various stages of life in your own childhood—times when you either felt the carefreeness and lack of responsibility inherent in childhood or, on the other hand, times when you felt helpless, powerless, or hurt as a child. Dreaming of an old man or woman typically represents useful experience accrued—in the form of insight, wisdom, and knowledge, for example.

If you dream of someone who is a particular age, don't discount the value of that specific number to other areas of your life, beyond your own chronological age. If necessary, also consider the number in other forms, and break it down using multiplication, division, addition, or subtraction. (See also *numbers*.)

air: Although some interpretations indicate that a dream of any sort of air has negative implications for the dreamer, it seems more likely that this is another instance where the quality or feeling of the dream element holds clues to its meaning. If, for example, the air is crisp and clear it probably points to something positive or agreeable that will happen. If the air is heavy or cloudy, on the other hand, this might symbolize a lack of clarity or certainty in your life, or an oppressive feeling that's hanging over you.

Additionally, air is one of the four primary elements and something that we can't live without. Therefore, don't overlook it as a symbol for something absolutely essential in your life.

Finally, pay attention to the puns and colloquialisms associated with this word. Do you need to "clear the air" with someone? Are you—or is someone you know—"full of hot air"? Or are you dealing with a person or situation that makes you feel like you have to "put on airs" or pretend to be something you're not?

airplane: Airplanes fly high in the sky, and dreaming you are in an airplane might indicate in a symbolic sense that you are soaring to new heights in a particular facet of your life. A dream of this sort can also imply you are taking a metaphorical journey into the unconscious. The higher view afforded in an airplane might also indicate that you are gaining a broader perspective on a situation. Additionally, an airplane dream can be a prelude to a flying dream or used as a launch pad to a lucid dream.

airport: In this case, thinking about what happens at airports and what you use them for will give you good clues to their meaning in your dreams. Airports are the places where travel begins—the starting point for new destinations and experiences. Therefore, it makes perfect sense to associate airports with change, transition, and the start of something different. Since we often stop over briefly at airports as we transfer from one flight to another, these places can also represent some sort of intermediate or in-between stage.

alarm: If you dream of an alarm ringing in warning, it indicates you have worries about some aspect of your life. Alarm clocks also sound each morning when it's time to rise and shine, so consider whether your dream of an alarm is suggesting that you are in need of a "wake-up call" in some area of your life.

alcohol: Different people have different associations when it comes to drinking alcohol. In some instances, having a few drinks is a fun, pleasurable experience that allows people to "loosen up" and relax a bit. When consumed excessively, however, alcoholic beverages dull the senses, inhibit mental clarity, and impair judgment. Pay attention to the overall feeling in your dream if it involves drinking alcohol: Why are you drinking, and where is the alcohol located in your dream, for example? Big-picture elements such as these will provide clues as to whether it holds negative or positive associations. (See also *drinking*.)

alien: In a general sense, aliens in a dream can represent fear of the unknown. Pay attention to your feelings toward the aliens in your dreams, though. If you dream that you encounter people from outer space and you feel strange around them, then strange things will start to happen in your life. If in your dream, however, you are positive toward the visitors from outer space, positive influences will be in your life.

alligator: This symbol may suggest that you're being thick-skinned or insensitive to someone else. It may also signify danger.

altar: An in-between place or bridge between the mundane and the eternal, an altar may quite possibly represent the need to give or receive by way of an offering. In fact, in ancient times, one of the earliest uses for altars was as a place to make sacrifices and offerings, so this image has a longstanding link with such associations. Today, in contemporary times, altars remain places central to worship, where people gather to be in the presence of the Divine together, and to share and take part in things such Communion, in the case of Christianity, for example. Consider, therefore, if there's any connection in your dream to this sort of mingling.

For many, houses of worship also serve as a reminder of repentance and, thus, in dreams altars might also provide a hint about not doing the wrong things.

Also, don't neglect to consider a play on words here: Is there anything in your life that has "altered" or is going to "alter" that is causing you concern?

amputation: To dream of losing a limb might symbolically represent a sense of losing or severing some other part of yourself in a more abstract way. If someone else in your dream has had a leg or arm amputated, that is a reflection of something they've been cut off from and, perhaps, something that you might have taken away or denied them.

amusement park: Dreaming of an amusement park might suggest that you need a vacation from your concerns about a troubling issue. To dream of being on a ride at an amusement park denotes an enjoyment of life and a feeling of being uninhibited.

anchor: An anchor symbolizes something that grounds you. It acts as your foundation and it also holds you in place. Depending on the context of the situation, this can be either beneficial or detrimental.

angels: Angels represent help from the higher self or from a guardian. The appearance of an angel in your dreams may suggest a growing spiritual awareness. Angels can also be symbolic of good health.

animals: Animals represent human beings' negative and positive qualities, and the wilder the animal, the more primitive the emotion. Animals also have very strong instincts; therefore, a dream of an animal might relate to your own instincts and intuition. Additionally, animals can relate to various sides of your "animal" nature, and dreaming of animals in general implies an awakening of the tribal soul (humans are, after all, animals too). In dreams, animals can also represent a guardian spirit, wisdom, innocence, predatory tendencies, or sexuality, depending on the perceived nature of the animal. An animal might additionally signify the physical body, or appear as a metaphor for an illness within the physical body.

Aggressive animals warn either of danger in your life or denote a sense of feeling threatened. Dreaming of an animal being tamed brings a warning to control your primal nature (for instance, to curb your overly exuberant physical passion). If an animal is killed in your dream, some type of literal or figurative death is going on around you.

ant: Ants suggest restlessness—in other words, feeling "antsy." They also signify small annoyances and irritations. Alternately, they may represent feelings of smallness or insignificance. If you dream of ants, consider the number of them present in the dream. Are you dreaming of a single ant, a colony, or a huge, swollen anthill?

If, in your dream, an ant is being crushed by a huge foot, ask yourself if you feel as if someone or something is squelching you. For example,

your industrious nature is being stunted by someone in a place of authority, or is someone purposefully trying to undermine your job?

apparition: An apparition can signify a message or warning. It can also be seen as communication with the dead. Alternately, you might feel
that another person in a relationship is like an apparition—someone who is there, but not truly
present.

apples: Apples stand for wholeness and for
knowledge, and a dream about apples generally
is a good dream. Ripe apples on a tree might
mean that your hope and hard work have borne
fruit, or that you are about to realize your dreams.
Red apples on a green-leafed tree mean good
news is coming your way. If the apples are ripe
on top of the tree, this is a warning not to aim too
high in your ambitions. If the apples are on the
ground, watch out for false friends. Dreaming of
decayed apples signifies that your efforts in your
financial endeavors are hopeless.

April: As April showers lead to May flowers,
to dream of this month represents that much
pleasure and fortune may be heading your way.

If the weather is bad, it may suggest the passing of bad luck.

arch: Passing under an arch in a dream may symbolize a transition in your life, a move from one phase or stage to another. If you avoid walking under the arch, the indication is that you are resisting transition or change. Note the shape of the arch, whether it's adorned in any way, or whether other people are also using it. This will flesh out the symbol for you.

arm: Arms allow you to hold and manipulate things in your everyday, waking environment, and the same can be true in a dream. Seeing an arm suggests that you can maneuver or manipulate things in your dream environment. If you flap your arms, it might indicate a desire to fly in your dream.

arrow: The Warrior's rune, the arrow is a call to action and discovery of personal power. Arrows are quick, precise tools and, therefore, imply skill and expertise.

ashes: Ashes are what's left of a substance after it's consumed by fire. Consider, therefore, if there is something in your life that can be equated with remnants or residual leftovers, whether it be from a relationship, situation, or anything else.

Additionally, ashes are a symbol of penance, as in the ashes smudged on the foreheads of Catholics on Ash Wednesday, at the start of Lent. Therefore, they might represent something you feel that you need to account or make up for.

Further, consider the words commonly recited at funerals—"Ashes to ashes, dust to dust . . ."—which allude back to Genesis 3:19, a passage that describes human beings returning to the ground, and to dust, when we die. Taken in this light, it's easy to recognize ashes as a symbol of mortality in our culture's collective consciousness.

Asia: If you dream of traveling to Asia, a change will happen in your life from which you will derive no material benefits.

athame: The ritual knife of Witchcraft, the athame represents the reality that tools are often double-edged and can be wielded to help or harm. This double-sided image could also apply to other situations—bear the old "double-edged sword" cliché in mind. (See also *sword*.)

atlas: Since atlases are large books containing a wide variety of maps, it makes sense that dreaming of an atlas would suggest that you are considering moving or taking a trip.

attack: A dream involving an attack falls into the fear/anxiety category. Whether the dream attack occurs in a frightening, surreal, or supernatural situation, or in a gritty, realistic scenario, some key points apply. Attack dreams always express a feeling of vulnerability, uncertainty, and powerlessness. Keep in mind that your behavior and responses when being attacked in a dream are just as important as those of the person or thing that is attacking you. Are you weak and unable to retaliate, or do you maintain your composure and stand up to your attacker?

In the instance of being attacked, consider whether there is something in your life that you feel the need to fight back against or defend yourself from. If, on the other hand, you are the one doing the attacking in the dream, look at things from the opposite side of the spectrum and consider whether or not you are the one inadvertently keeping someone else down.

attic: If you dream of entering an attic, you may be exploring the realm of the higher self or seeking knowledge there. An attic can also represent a place where things are hidden or stored from the past. The dream might be suggesting that you need to take some part of yourself out of hiding or that you should dispose of the things in your past to which you are clinging.

August: Dreaming of August may suggest unfortunate dealings in business and love. If a young woman dreams that she will be wed in this month, it is an omen of sorrow to come in her early married life.

aunt: Dreaming of your extended family is not always a good omen. If a woman dreams of her aunt, she will soon receive severe criticism of choices and actions she makes in life.

autumn: Autumn is a time of ripeness, fullness, and harvest, a time to reap what has been sown. If you dream of this season, consider if there is a project, relationship, or situation in your life that has, after much nurturing, work, and cultivation, reached its fullest potential.

avalanche: Dreaming of an avalanche can signify a large obstacle in your path—something that might feel, perhaps, as if it's burying you. Keep in mind that avalanches have a cumulative effect: They pick up more snow, debris, and speed as they go along. Consequently, If you dream of an avalanche, consider whether there is a situation in your life that is "snowballing" in this way.

B

baby: A baby in a dream may represent an idea that is gestating or growing. It could also relate to the pending birth of a child or a desire for a family. Alternately, a baby could indicate dependent behavior or infantile longings. A baby walking alone indicates independence. A bright, clean baby represents requited love and many warm friends.

back: When your back is turned, you are unaware of what might sneak up on you, and you can't see what's going on. Therefore, this symbol indicates a sense of vulnerability or lack of control. Your backbone is another associated element, and having a "backbone" (or not) figuratively implies a sense of courage, resolution, strength of character, determination, and strong will. Other related analogies include "backing off" or giving yourself space from a situation; being "stabbed in the back" or betrayed by someone; and the desire for "backup" or support.

balcony: A balcony might stand for the public part of the personality. The condition of the balcony has a lot to do with the symbol's meaning. If it's clean and polished, the dream indicates that others hold you in high regard. If it's a crumbling, tarnished balcony, it might suggest that you need to repair your public image.

balloon: Generally, balloons are a positive symbol, since they are typically used as festive decorations to mark happy, celebratory occasions such as birthdays, holidays, and baby and wedding showers. They also represent a feeling of lightness or floating. If the balloon pops in your dream, however, this is not a good sign. In this case, it might be an indication of a hope or aspiration that has been thwarted.

bank: Generally, a bank is a symbol of security and power—a foundation—but the meaning depends on what you're doing in the bank. If you are receiving or depositing money, it's usually an auspicious sign, an indication that you are financially secure. If you are waiting in line, it literally may mean waiting for a check or money to arrive. Likewise, if you're holding up a bank, it may symbolize that money you're expecting is being "held up" or delayed.

baptism: Baptism is a key ritual in Christian faiths and it signifies a restoration of the purity and innocence of humankind before Adam and Eve's sin. Baptism can be symbolic of many things, including consecration, renewal, figurative rebirth, cleansing from sin or negativity, and fresh beginnings. If you dream of baptism, consider if there is something from which you feel the need to be cleansed or some sin or wrongdoing you hope to be forgiven for. Also consider any new undertakings that are changing or redefining your life as you have previously known it.

basement: Dreaming of being in a basement might indicate that you are connecting with the subconscious mind. You might possibly be unearthing something hidden in your past that you need to examine. A dream of a basement could also signify that your pleasure and prosperous possibilities might lessen or even develop into trouble. (See also *underground*.)

bat: Bats are creatures that have an amazing ability to maneuver through dark places like caves with much agility in flight. Therefore, a dream of a bat suggests making your way through an uncertain situation successfully. Alternatively, this symbol might represent improved luck and happiness.

bathroom: Dreaming of being in a bathroom might simply mean that your bladder is full. It could also symbolize a place of privacy. If the bathroom is crowded, the dream might indicate you feel as if you lack privacy in your life. If you find yourself in a bathroom meant for the opposite sex, it might suggest that you are crossing boundaries. A bathroom dream can also relate to the elimination of something in your life.

beach: Beaches are often idyllic places that conjure images of sun, sand, and soothing waves. They often elicit feelings of tranquility, peacefulness, and even rejuvenation. Not surprisingly, therefore, a dream of a beach can be indicative of rest and relaxation. Looking at it from the opposing viewpoint, in fact, a vivid dream of a beautiful beach might stand in stark contrast to the hectic, busy pace of your everyday life, indicating a need to slow down and get away from it all.

bear: Dreaming of a bear might speak of your mood (if you've been bearish). The bear traditionally symbolizes forbearance, protectiveness, fearlessness, and possibly the need to rest up in preparation for a draining situation.

bee: A bee's sting is sharp and often sneaks up on you when you least expect it. Therefore, a dream of bees might indicate a feeling of being hurt, or a fear that you might get hurt. These creatures are also hard workers that fly from flower to flower gathering pollen to make honey. In this context, they can be a symbol of industriousness, productivity, and success.

beetle: As with most insects, which are generally considered bothersome, nasty, or dirty creatures, beetles represent unpleasant things in dreams for the most part. However, because the scarab beetle was venerated in Ancient Egypt and considered a source of protection, beetles can also signify this element in dreams.

beggar: Figuratively speaking, dreaming of a beggar indicates a lack, a feeling of falling short or not succeeding, or a sense of being in need. In a more literal sense, however, a beggar is a symbol of those less fortunate and might be an indication of a concern for the poor or a need to be of help. Also, if you are the beggar in your dream, it might be an indication that you will be receiving help when you need it.

bells: A message of protection or warning, bells might also be an advisory that you need to center and focus. Alternately, dreaming of bells tolling might mean a distant friend will die. If you dream of a joyous bell ringing, however, expect success in all aspects of your life.

beryl: This stone predicts that a happy relationship is on the horizon for the dreamer.

bier: If you dream of a bier—the flowers placed on a coffin—no matter how fresh and beautiful the flowers are, you will know losses.

birds: The symbolic value changes according to the specific bird. Generally, however, birds are a positive sign. They represent liberation, movement, and the ability to distance yourself from a situation. The appearance of a bird in a dream could relate to a wish for freedom, to fly away, or to flee from something. Birds can also be spiritual symbols. Among certain Native American tribes, an eagle symbolizes spiritual knowledge. A vulture might symbolize death, and a hummingbird might point to a matter accelerating or to the tendency to flit from one thing to another.

More Bird-Related Symbols

There are many symbols associated with birds that might creep into your dreams. The specifics of the situation will hold insight into the meaning of the dream. Here are a few more specific examples of birds in dreams:

Birds flying: If either a man or a woman dreams of flying birds, it's usually interpreted to mean prosperity is to come.

Bird's nest: Dreaming of a bird's nest filled with eggs means good things will soon follow. To dream of an empty bird's nest denotes gloomy days ahead in business.

Birds of prey: There is a scheming person out to injure you if you dream of vultures. This evildoer will not succeed, however, if you dream the vulture is dead. A woman dreaming of a vulture indicates she will soon be overwhelmed by slander and gossip.

A bird that's singing happily foretells success in its song. If you dream of songless birds, on the other hand, watch out: Trouble could be coming your way.

birth: Dreaming of a birth can signify great joy. The act of literally birthing a baby in a dream often represents some sort of figurative birth in waking life. For example, it can be the completion of some sort of creative work or project that has involved great labor. A birthing dream might also signify a new side of yourself that is emerging, or "being born." (See also *giving birth*.)

birthday: Birthday dreams can have contrary meanings depending on the context. To dream of receiving birthday presents may mean happy surprises or advancements are in order. For an older person to dream of a birthday may signify long hardship and sorrow; to the young it is a symbol of poverty.

bleeding: Blood is vital to life, and to dream of bleeding suggests a loss of power and a change for the worse in fortune. Blood is also an indication of a wound or injury. Although this might appear in a dream as a literal wound, it might signify some sort of emotional wound or mental scar you are carrying in your waking life.

blessing: To dream of receiving a blessing is a positive sign, as blessings signify favor and approval.

blindfold: If you are blindfolded in a dream, it indicates that someone is trying to deceive you or prevent you from seeing something clearly.

Conversely, if you are the one doing the blind-folding, consider whether you are trying to pull the wool over someone else's eyes.

blindness: Blindness in a dream suggests the inability or unwillingness to face something in life or to see a person, situation, or some other cir-cumstance for what it really is.

blossoms: A dream that involves blossoming flowers implies fulfillment and the opening of new skills, either magical or mundane. Blossoms also symbolize hope and potential.

boat: In dreams, boats usually represent life's voyage.

bomb: A dream of a bomb typically repre-sents some sort of volatile situation that is in dan-ger of blowing up. Pay attention to what is going on in this dream. If, for example, you are han-dling a bomb with care or trying to defuse it, this implies a potentially difficult situation that needs to be dealt with gently or cautiously.

book: Books represent knowledge, informa-tion, and understanding. Pay attention to the age of the book. If it is an old book, for example, the knowledge might come in the form of wisdom from those who have more life experience than you. If the book is pristine and unused, this could be a symbol of new knowledge soon to come your way. Dreaming of a sacred text, such as the Bible or Koran, might indicate spiritual insight and knowledge.

bouquet: Happy circumstances are denoted when dreaming of bouquets, especially if they are made up of richly colored flowers. A legacy from an unknown and wealthy relative might soon be yours. In addition there will probably be a pleasant gathering of young folks in your life.

brain: The brain is the center of mental processes and intelligence, and to dream of this organ is telling you something about your own ways of thinking, or perhaps the thinking of others. Depending on the circumstances, this sort of dream could indicate that you need to give things more thought or consideration or, on the other hand, that things might be weighing too heavily on your mind and you're overly concerned.

breasts: Women's breasts might relate to sexual desire. They can also symbolize nurturing, motherhood, or a concern about exposure. Always consider what's going on in relation to the symbol, and pay attention to things such as whether or not the breasts are exposed, or if they are diseased or injured.

bride: It's good news if you dream of a bride—whether you are the bride or it's your uncle's step-cousin's daughter. To dream of a bride denotes you will soon come into a big inheritance. If in your dream a man kisses the bride, that denotes a happy reconciliation between family and friends.

bridge: Since a bridge connects you from one place to another, in dreaming it might represent a crossing from one state of mind to another. Consider the other elements in the dream. Are you crossing dangerous waters? What's waiting for you at the other side of the bridge? What's behind you?

briefcase: Briefcases typically contain papers related to work. Therefore, says author Gayle Delaney, individuals who have retired or who have been fired from their jobs sometimes have dreams involving this carrying case. But the shift in your work life does not necessarily have to be so momentous. If you dream of a briefcase, also look at other circumstances going on in your career, to ascertain what this symbol might represent.

brother: Since the family is the primary unit of stability and security from the time you are a child, any dream of a close family member can conjure these associations. A dream of a sibling, however, might not only indicate this sense of love and closeness, but also the typical pull of "sibling rivalry" at the same time. More specifically, an older brother might indicate a figure of authority, while a younger brother might represent a more vulnerable role. (See also *sister.*)

bull: In dreams, bulls signify masculine energy, stubbornness, creativity, leadership skills, the ego/self (especially for men), and moving forward too quickly and doing damage in the process. If you dream of a bull, consider the circumstances. If, for example, a bull is killed by a matador (who happens to look like you), a possible interpretation might be that you are getting your bull-headed nature (and temper) under firm control.

bus: In general, dreaming of travel can relate to an actual upcoming trip. But if you have no plans for a journey, your dream sojourn might be a symbolic one. Pay particular attention to details about your trip. A bus can be a vehicle for moving ahead to one's goal. If you're traveling with others, you could be on a collective journey. If you dream of a bus, notice other aspects of the dream, such as the luggage you're carrying, your destination, and what you're leaving behind. Where are you going? Are you traveling alone or with others? Do you have luggage with you? Keep in mind that what happens on your trip might be more important than the destination.

buttercup: Dreaming of buttercup flowers represents business success.

butterfly: Brightly colored and beautiful, these graceful insects suggest feelings of happiness, lightness, freedom, and flight. On a deeper level, butterflies, which undergo a metamorphosis from their caterpillar state, signify transition, transformation, and movement from one phase of life to the other. (See also *caterpillar*.)

buzzard: If you dream of a buzzard, watch out. An old scandal is likely to surface and injure your reputation. If in your dream a buzzard is sitting on a railroad, you might experience an accident or loss in the near future. Should the buzzard in your dream fly away, all your troubles will be resolved!

cage: A cage represents possession or control, and what you see in the cage is the key to interpreting this sign. A cage full of birds could signify great wealth and many children, while a single bird may represent a successful marriage or mate. An empty cage might mean the loss of a family member, while a cage full of wild animals might signify that you have control over a particular aspect of your life and that you will triumph over misfortune.

cake: A cake might symbolize that a celebration is at hand. Typically eaten during or at the end of rituals like birthdays and weddings, cakes represent wishes, an initiation, or other sacred rites. Or perhaps there's something in your life worth celebrating that you have overlooked.

camel: Camels are animals who have evolved and adapted to living in extreme conditions while running on meager reserves. If you dream of a camel, therefore, prepare for a time of stretched resources.

canal: Canals suggest a journey through the unconscious. Pay attention to other details in the dream. Is the water muddy or clear? Are you traveling with friends or family?

cancer: Dreaming of cancer doesn't mean you have it or are going to get it. To be successfully treated for cancer in a dream signals a change for the better. Dreaming of cancer may also symbolize a desperate or foreboding situation, or a draining of resources.

candles: Usually something of a spiritual nature is suggested by the appearance of candles in dreams. A candle provides light in the dark, or guidance through dark matters or through the unknown and, hence, represents enlightenment in dreams. The flame of a candle can also signify the light that shines within each soul.

The contextual meaning of a candle can be interpreted through its behavior in your dream. If a candle burns down to nothingness, it might indicate a fear or concern about death or impotence. A candle being extinguished could indicate a feeling of being overworked. A steadily burning candle might signify a steadfast character and constancy in friends and family.

canoe: Canoes suggest a short journey that requires some effort, but that is often pleasantly tranquil. Pay attention to other elements in the dream, such as the state of the water and how hard you are paddling. A dream of paddling on a calm stream symbolizes confidence in your own abilities. If the river is shallow and quick, the dream may indicate concern over a hasty decision in a recent matter. To dream of rowing with your paramour might indicate an imminent and lasting marriage, but if the waters are rough, then perhaps some effort is required before you are ready to marry.

car: A moving car may mean you are headed toward a goal or moving ahead. If you're in the driver's seat, a car can symbolize taking charge of your life. Is there a "backseat driver" in the vehicle? Or are you taking the backseat in some situation in your life? Being a passenger indicates that someone else might be controlling a situation. A stolen or lost car could indicate that you are losing control of your life. Cars sometimes represent the physical body, so take note of the car's condition. Is it rusting? Does the exterior shine? How does the interior look?

carnation: Carnations signify love in dreams.

carnelian: In dreams, the stone carnelian suggests that luck is on the horizon.

carousel: To dream of riding a carousel suggests that you are going round in circles and not making any progress in your endeavors. Seeing others ride a carousel symbolizes unfulfilled ambitions.

castle: Seeing one of these majestic structures in a dream might suggest power, strength, security, and protection. Castles in the sky are fantasies and illusions, wishes to escape from one's present circumstances.

cat: Cats can have both positive and negative attributes, depending on your association with them and the surrounding circumstances in the dream. Cats can mean prosperity or quick and agile recuperation. They can also represent independence, the feminine, or sexual prowess. Kittens can mean new ideas, and if you dream of a kitten in a basement it might signify ideas arising from the unconscious mind. Additionally, since cats see well in the dark, they can signify an ability to find illumination in an obscured situation. Dreaming of cats isn't always positive, however: They might symbolize evil or bad luck, or a catty or cunning person. (See also *kitten* and *owl*.)

caterpillar: Like its ultimate form, the butterfly, the caterpillar represents change and transition as you move from one stage of life to another. (See also *butterfly*.)

cattle: To dream of healthy, contented cattle grazing in a green pasture suggests prosperity and happiness. Conversely, dreaming of weak, poorly fed cattle suggests you are spending your energy unwisely. Stampeding cattle implies that something in your life is out of control.

cauldron: Because a cauldron has three legs, witches associate it with the threefold Goddess and her influence. With this in mind, in dreams, a cauldron also represents traditional feminine qualities, such as fertility and rebirth, and other attributes, including wisdom, rejuvenation, nurturing, creativity, and insight.

cave: Caves can be dark, hidden areas, and often represent an obstacle in dreams. If you can find your way out of one in your dream, this indicates that you'll be able to solve the problem at hand or overcome your obstacle. If, on the other hand, you are lost in a cave, it suggests that you still have a way to go when it comes to working out the situation.

cellar: A cellar often symbolizes the unconscious mind, a place where knowledge is stored or hidden. It can also indicate that the dream comes from the deepest levels of your unconscious, so pay special attention to the way the cellar is lit and to colors and textures. If you dream you are in a cold, damp cellar, it denotes you will soon be oppressed by doubts.

chameleon: Chameleons change color, which indicates transformation. A chameleon's shifting hues help it to blend in with its surroundings, so dreaming of this creature also indicates a knowledge of when to remain quiet and out of sight.

chariot: Riding in a chariot in a dream suggests positive news or success in a matter.

chase: If you dream of being chased, it is usually an indication that your life (at least according to your unconscious) is not up to par and it's coming back around to get you. In most cases, it doesn't matter who is after you, whether it's your mother-in-law or big, hairy orange monsters. Study the characters in your dreams for clues to help you determine what it is you are really running away from in real life.

chasm: Related to other dream images of a void, this notion relates back to the fear of falling into something dangerously unknown or empty. This dream can represent obstacles, uncertainty, and also fear of failure, of your capability, or whatever else is concerning you. (See also *abyss*, *cliff*, *pit*, and *precipice*.)

cheese: Dreaming of cheese generally indicates that sorrow lies ahead. If you dream of Swiss cheese, on the other hand, this suggests you will come into substantial possessions and have good health.

chicken: To dream of a brood of chickens denotes that although you have many cares that cause you worries, you will profit from some of that worry. If you dream of young chicks, you will be very successful in all your enterprises.

children: If dreaming of children, you might possibly be yearning to return to a simpler, less complicated life. Such dreams might also relate to a desire to return to the past to recapture good times or to satisfy unfulfilled hopes. According to Dr. Ann Faraday, in dreams, children can also represent "underdeveloped parts of ourselves," those parts of ourselves that are still trying to re-solve issues from childhood. Dreams of children are also likely to arise when you are faced with something unfamiliar or unknown. If you dream of a child, consider whether you've recently started something new that you don't know very much about.

chocolate: Chocolate suggests a need or a desire to indulge in something, perhaps a forbidden something. It can also indicate a need to limit your indulgences.

church: You might think that dreaming of houses of worship would indicate peace and happiness, but the world of dreams can some-times be surprising. If you dream of seeing a church off in the distance, a long awaited event will be disappointing. Dreaming of entering a church in a gloomy mood can mean you should expect some sadness in the near future.

circle: Generally, circles represent a sense of forever or eternity, since they have no beginning and no end. They can also relate to interconnection, as in "the circle of life." In Jungian terms, a circle represents the Self and wholeness. It can also relate to a symbol of protection or social connections, as in a "circle" of friends. If you're "circling around something," caution is indicated. Freudian interpretation holds that the circle represents the vagina and sexual desire. Other associations connected with circles include a sense of sacred space, completion, wholeness, equity, and cycles.

classroom: Often, a classroom dream relates to a personal growth period you are going through. If you dream of finding yourself in a classroom, examine your surroundings and your reason for being there. Is there a positive feeling about the learning environment? Do you recognize who is teaching the class and the subject matter? If you are a teacher having a classroom dream, pay particular attention to what is going on in your everyday classroom life, because the meaning of this dream might be more practical than symbolic.

Orientation

The following classroom dream was told by a thirty-three-year-old woman who had recently joined a dream group. The dream had occurred eleven years earlier, when she was in college, and it had always puzzled her.

Tanya and I are sitting in a lobby with perhaps a dozen other people of various ages and races. We aren't sure why we're there. There's nothing about the lobby to tell me exactly where it is. I feel very uneasy about this place. I go up to the information desk and ask the receptionist what we're waiting for.

"For the class to begin," she replies.

"I didn't sign up for a class," I tell her.

"You must have. You're here."

Then she goes back to whatever she was doing, and I return to my seat. Not long afterward, she calls my name and Tanya's and we file into a college-style auditorium. It's crowded with people and brightly lit by a skylight. The color of the sky is odd, a kind of glowing cerulean blue.

The speaker is a well-known literary figure (whose name I forgot when I woke), but whom I know died some years before. I suddenly realize I am in an afterlife classroom, about to be oriented to dying and to whatever happens next.

This dream recurs periodically, usually when the woman experiences a "crisis of faith" in her spiritual beliefs. Each time she experiences the dream, it always renews her belief in the path she has chosen.

cliff: This dream is related to other symbols related to falling over the edge into something unknown or empty. It can represent obstacles, uncertainty, and also fear of failure, of your capability, and anything else you are unsure about. (See also *abyss*, *chasm*, *pit*, and *precipice*.)

clock: Who isn't acutely aware of the way in which time seems to fly by? Given that our modern life is so tied to "watching the clock," as we constantly attempt to adhere to our monthly, daily, and even hourly schedules, it's no surprise that a dream of a clock symbolizes the passage of time. Pay attention to the details and context clues in a dream of this sort, because the broad scope of time can apply to anything from growing older to an internal clock you might not be realizing you've set for yourself. Do you have certain expectations about when and how soon you would like to accomplish certain things? Could your dream be a subtle reminder to pick up the pace in certain areas, or lighten up in others? (See also *watch*.)

closet: Closets are places where things are stored or hidden. If there is something you are hiding in your life, your dream might possibly indicate that it is time to release whatever it is.

clouds: Dark, stormy clouds rolling in at a low altitude accompanied by flashing lightning might represent your anger regarding a situation. A slate-gray clouded sky might indicate that your views are clouded on a subject. Think about what there is in your life that needs clarity. Dreaming of white, billowing clouds floating in a blue sky suggests that matters are clearing up.

coffee: Whether it's Starbucks or Dunkin' Donuts, if you dream of drinking coffee, it denotes that your friends disapprove of your marriage intentions. That's assuming you have marriage intentions. If you are already married and you dream of drinking coffee, be prepared for many disagreements and quarrels. If you dream you are roasting coffee, you soon will marry a stranger. To dream of ground coffee signifies you will be successful in overcoming some adversity.

coffeehouse: To dream of visiting a coffeehouse denotes that women are conspiring against you and your possessions. This is true whether a man or woman has this dream.

coffin: A coffin might symbolize a feeling of confinement. Coffins also relate to death; in this case, ask yourself what part of your life might be dead or dying.

college: College represents distinction and the attainment of your hopes through hard work. To dream of a college might suggest that you will advance to a position long sought after. Dreaming that you are back in college suggests that distinction will follow a period of hard work.

corpse: To dream of yourself as a corpse or to experience your death is not necessarily a prediction of your demise. It could signify a major change in your life, such as the ending of a long-held job or a divorce. If you dream of killing yourself, it could mean that you are going through a traumatic personal transformation, leaving your old life behind. (See also *suicide*.)

cousin: To dream of members of your extended family is not always portentous. Dreaming of a cousin indicates you might have disappointment and sadness. Even dreaming of a friendly correspondence with your cousin signifies that there might be a major falling-out in the family.

cow: A cow can represent fertility, sustenance, or even prosperity. Alternately, a cow might signify a desire for sexual intercourse, or a fear of being unable to resist engaging in sex.

crab: Dreaming of a crab signifies moodiness or misdirection, as well as situations that seem to lead nowhere. On another level, crabs are creatures that don't move forward in a straight way; rather, they move sideways. Therefore, if you dream of a crab, ask yourself if there is something in your life that you aren't confronting head-on. Are you skirting around the issue?

crash: At first glance, a crash that occurs in a dream might seem alarming, frightening, and full of destructive implications. However, dreaming of this symbol does not necessarily imply something negative. In fact, it might denote an important event or accomplishment. Dream crashes can also represent something startling, noticeable, or worthy of attention.

cream: To dream of cream portends wealth. Dreaming of drinking cream means good fortune.

creek: A creek represents a short journey or a new experience. Are you exploring a creek with a friend? Is the creek muddy? Note the other aspects of the dream.

crocodile: In dreams, a crocodile represents lies or misrepresentation.

cross or crucifix: In Christian tradition, the cross is a symbol of suffering and of burdens to be carried. However, despite the grief and pain that is endured, the cross ultimately symbolizes triumph over adversity.

crossroads: If you have arrived at a crossroads in your dream, this indicates the need to make a choice. If you are hesitant to take either path, this suggests indecision in some matter. In that case, this is a clear indication that making a choice and moving forward is better than standing still without progress.

crown: The obvious definition is wealth, position, power, and authority. But is the crown something desired or feared in the dream? Is it within reach or escaping your grasp?

crystal: Dreaming of a clear crystal represents clarity, either in your thoughts or psychically. If you dream of a lone crystal and the stone shatters, this implies that a very difficult emotional or physical situation might be on the horizon. This situation could, in fact, be one that has the potential to be shattering to your sense of confidence or self.

crystal ball: If you dream of someone seeing your fortune in a crystal ball, that indicates you are contemplating some complicated events in your life. Use caution. For a young woman to have this dream indicates she is trying to make the best choice between two men.

cyclops: Beware of dreaming of one eye—it portends that watchful enemies will ferret out a chance to do you harm in your business. Dreaming of a one-eyed man indicates loss and trouble with others plotting against you in your business.

daffodil: The daffodil is one of the first flowers to pop up through the ground at the end of the winter. Consequently, this bright, striking flower represents the renewal and new life of spring.

dancing: A dream that involves dancing suggests integration or participation in something greater than yourself. Pay attention to where and with whom you are dancing in the dream to gain more insight into its meaning. A dream dance evokes movement, freedom, joy, and a time of happiness and levity.

darkness: Darkness is a symbol of the unconscious, the hidden, and the unknown. Darkness can also stand for evil, death, and fear. To dream of being overtaken by darkness suggests fear or trepidation over a matter at hand. To dream that you lose a friend or child in the darkness symbolizes that you may be provoked from many different sources.

Darkness represents a lack of illumination, and this can apply in the figurative sense to some aspect of your life. It can signify anything from a situation you're depressed about, to a transition stage as you're becoming accustomed to something new—somewhat akin to "feeling your way around in the dark." A dream of darkness can also relate to a feeling of not being in touch with something, as in being "in the dark" about it.

daughter: To dream of a daughter when you don't have one might simply be an indication of your desire for children. If you do have a daughter, in your dreams she might represent elements of yourself as a child, or your own sense of responsibility as a parent. (See also *son*.)

daybreak: Seeing the break of the new day in a dream symbolizes that the outlook is brightening on a matter. A gloomy or cloudy day suggests bad luck in a new enterprise.

dead: The appearance of the dead in a dream typically signifies a warning of some kind. To see the dead living and happy represents a bad influence that may be affecting your life. (See also *death* and *dying*.)

death: Death is the ultimate metamorphosis, the passage from one state of being to another. In the tarot, the Death card means transformation, a major change that hurls you from one way of life to another. In a dream, death is usually a symbol for the same thing.

Only rarely do death dreams portend actual physical death. Many times, dreams about death are simply metaphors for major changes happening in life. These sorts of dreams might be symbolic of your relationships, work, or aspects of personality. When you have such a dream, you need to consider whether an area of your life is undergoing transformation. Are you in the middle of a divorce? About to have a baby? Are you about to get married? Are you considering a career change? In this sense, death dreams are not so much about death—they're more about the rebirth that comes from moving from one, old stage of life, to another stage, as you progress to a new level.

A death or near-death dream involving a living family member or relative, like most death dreams, might be pointing to a major upheaval in that person's life. In that case, the dream acts as a conduit of information.

When dreaming of a friend or relative who has already died, don't worry. This isn't an omen that you or anyone else you know is going to die. It might just simply mean that there are parts of

Death Dreams and Other Symbols

Quite often, dreams about death involve other symbols, like a car, which is a perfect dream metaphor for where you're going in life and how the journey is unfolding. For a sixteen-year-old girl, for example, a death dream in which a car figured prominently underscored the recent move her family made from the state where she'd been born and raised. For a forty-eight-year-old accountant, a death dream symbolized a major job transition from a large firm to self-employment.

In the following dream, the death symbolism pointed to a young man's changing feelings about his girlfriend:

Jan and I are at the carnival that's rolled into town. It was her idea to go and she's like a kid, eating cotton candy, running from ride to ride, insistent that I go with her. I don't like carnivals and wish we could leave.

She wants to go on the roller coaster, I don't. We argue out there in front of everyone and I'm totally embarrassed. Just to keep her quiet, I relent and go on the roller coaster with her.

I hate the roller coaster, everyone screaming, Jan clutching my arm and shrieking like a five-year-old. As our car speeds down one of the hills in the track, Jan's seat restraint suddenly snaps open and she's hurled out of the car. I see her shooting like a missile through the air and know it's going to kill her. I feel relieved.

When I woke up, I was shocked at my lack of emotion and couldn't go back to sleep. But the longer I lay there, the clearer it became that she and I no longer enjoyed the same things, that she was immature, and that for me the relationship was already over. Ending it was merely a formality.

this person's personality that have bearing on your own life. If you dream of your grandfather who has already passed on, for example, and the first thing that comes to mind when you think of him is what a hard worker he was, perhaps this is a subtle message that you need to buckle down more in your own endeavors.

Occasionally, a death dream might indicate a death, but not necessarily the death of a person. If there's no sense of fear in the death, the dream can mean you're letting go of something or moving on. On the other hand, a corpse can indicate a lifeless routine. (See also *dead* and *dying*.)

🔆 Transitional Symbols

As described in the entry above, death is not a literal symbol, but rather a more abstract representation of a difficult transition or upheaval taking place in life. Some other dream symbols that also convey a similar feeling include war, graves, stench, rats, and leeches. ◗

December: A time of gift giving and receiving, to dream of this month can suggest the accumulation of wealth and fortune.

deer: A deer in a dream might symbolize hunting. Deer are also graceful and gentle creatures who are easily frightened. In folklore, deer are the messengers of fairies and, therefore, can be seen as messengers of the unconscious. Deer might also represent swift legal movement.

delight: Dreaming about being in a state of delight—feeling keen enjoyment—means also that all aspects of your life will go well and you will be successful.

desert: A desert is usually thought of as a desolate place, where little grows. It can be symbolic of a fear of death, or of being barren. But a desert can also symbolize hidden beauty and hidden life that is camouflaged to ordinary perceptions.

devil: The quintessential symbol of evil and temptation, if you see the devil in your dreams in his stereotypical form with the usual trappings, it could mean you're hiding something wrong that you've done and your guilty conscience is bothering you. If you are fighting the devil off, this might represent people who are trying to hurt you.

dew: Suggestive of tiny treasures or small pleasures, to dream of sparkling dew may represent that wealth and achievement are due. For a single person, perhaps a fortunate marriage is imminent.

diamonds: When you dream of diamonds, a lot depends on the context and the other symbols present in the dream—not to mention your own personal impressions of those symbols and the diamond within that construct. Typical interpretations vary, and diamonds have come to symbolize a variety of things, from love, devotion, and faithfulness (as in a diamond engagement and wedding ring); to forbearance and strength; to good luck, victory, success, and zeal; and even money.

If you dream of owning diamonds, you will have great honor bestowed on you—great honor from high places. A gift of a diamond depends on who's giving it and other circumstances. A diamond received from a parent or relative could relate to an inheritance; if given by a friend, it might indicate a wish to obtain that person's love. Women dreaming of receiving a diamond or diamonds from a lover denotes they will make a great marriage and be happy and wealthy. If you dream you lose a diamond, however, look out for disgrace and need. A lost diamond, especially a ring, can also symbolize a concern about a love relationship.

digging: What are you digging for? If it's something lost, you might be attempting to retrieve a part of your past. If it's a treasure, you might be delving into the unconscious, a treasure-house of knowledge. If, however, you are burying something, it indicates a wish to cover up an act, hide your feelings, or hide the facts of the matter.

disinheritance: Not surprisingly, dreaming of disinheritance denotes loss and rough times.

divination tools: These tools represent the need to examine something closely or gather more information.

diving: To dream of diving into a body of water might indicate that you are about to dive into something related to your waking life. On a deeper level, a diving dream could symbolize an exploration of the unconscious. From a Freudian perspective, such a dream suggests the dreamer is diving into a new sexual relationship.

doctor: A doctor can represent a healing guide or indicate that healing is taking place. For some people, a doctor in a dream might symbolize mainstream thinking as opposed to alternative health options. Doctors are also people who provide help when you need it, so also consider if this interpretation fits with something going on in your life. Is there some situation in which you are unknowingly seeking help? (See also *physician* and *nurse*.)

dog: Since the loyal dog is "Man's Best Friend," it's no surprise that in dreams, dogs represent steadfast friends or companions. Dreaming of a dog can also mean that you're seeking companionship, affection, or loyalty. If in your dream the dog bites, it might indicate a feeling of disloyalty. To hear dogs barking suggests a message or a warning from your unconscious.

dolphins: Since these creatures reside in the sea, dolphins might be considered guides to the unconscious realms and messengers of the unconscious. Dreaming of a dolphin might also suggest rapid movement and decision-making; it could also represent a message that requires attention.

door: A common dream symbol, doors can indicate an opening or a new opportunity at hand. A closed door suggests that something is inaccessible or hidden. If a door is broken, there might be something hindering you from the new opportunity. The condition of the door, the material from which it's made, and any markings that appear on it often provide clues about what lies behind a closed door. (See also *gate*.)

doorbell: If you dream you hear a doorbell ringing, expect to be called away to visit a friend or relative in need.

dove: Doves are a symbol of peace and tranquility. Additionally, since doves are birds that mate for life, this symbol indicates lasting love and a happy domestic situation.

dragonfly: In dreams, dragonflies indicate improved health or fortune, or a balancing of the head and heart.

drinking: Drinking water in a dream might simply mean that you are thirsty. Symbolically, water is related to the unconscious and emotions. Drinking may suggest you are being nourished or have a thirst for emotional involvement. Drinking alcoholic beverages can symbolize a sense of feeling high about a matter. As a metaphor, the drinking of "spirits" might suggest a search for spiritual sustenance. For an alcoholic or someone close to an alcoholic, a dream of drinking alcohol might be a warning. (See also *alcohol*.)

drought: Generally an unfavorable omen in a dream, droughts represent the absence of life or the drying up of your emotions. Are you with someone in the dream? Then maybe there is an unresolved issue between you and someone you are close to that is leading to a quarrel or separation.

drum: Dreaming of a drum or drumbeats might relate to a primitive urge. Alternately, a drum possibly symbolizes communication, magic, or even an entrepreneurial spirit—as in drumming up business.

dusk: Dusk denotes the end of the day; the end of happiness or clarity on an issue, or a dark outlook on a matter at hand.

dwarf: Dwarfs are traditionally associated with magical powers. Dreaming of a dwarf could be an extremely fortuitous sign. On the other hand, a dwarf can symbolize a stunted condition. If growth is limited, alternate paths must be pursued.

dying: Dreams of dying represent the ending of an emotional state or situation at hand. To dream that you are going to die suggests an inattention to a particular aspect of your life. To see animals in the throes of death symbolizes bad influences are a threat. (See also *dead* and *death*.)

E

eagle: The eagle, soaring through the sky, can symbolize a spiritual quest. Traditionally, eagles were associated with nobility. This bird can also stand for combat, pride, courage, and ferocity. Additionally, eagles can symbolize a father figure, the sun/solar energy, freedom, difficult goals, and authority.

ears: To dream of human ears can be a warning to watch out what you say. Ears can also call attention to the need to listen carefully to what's going on around you.

earthquake: Dreaming of an earthquake might suggest that personal, financial, or business matters are unstable. Is there something upsetting taking place in your life? Earthquakes can also have sexual connotations, such as the desire for sexual release. If there are others in the dream, does one of them make the "earth move" for you?

eating: A dream of eating might suggest a desire or craving for love or power. It can mean you are enjoying life or indulging in its pleasures. If you are the one being eaten in the dream, ask yourself if something is "eating at you." Do you feel as if you are being eaten alive?

eclipse: An eclipse suggests a disruption of the normal. When something is "eclipsed," it signifies a period of activity has ended. An eclipse also speaks of being in a sort of limbo, often between two different phases of life. Also, an eclipse can mean that cosmic forces might be at work in your life. For instance, a lunar eclipse is a warning that you might be trying to run from magickal arts or abilities. Conversely, a solar eclipse speaks of someone who doesn't put the proper foundations behind his or her beliefs and tries to hide from the light of reason.

ecstasy: To dream of ecstasy—that feeling of overwhelming, rapturous delight—portends you will have a visit from a long, absent friend.

eel: An eel can be a phallic symbol. Its movement through water contains sexual overtones. Take your cues from what the eel is doing.

egg: In the Freudian interpretation, eggs can symbolize the male testicles and stand for virility. In the Jungian view, eggs represent wholeness, fertility, and new life. Eggs can also represent un-hatched ideas; finding a nest of eggs might indicate a waiting period, or that ideas are gestating. Also think about the context of the dream. Is someone "egging" you on, for instance?

elephant: The appearance of these large, solid animals may portend the possession of wealth, honor, and a steadfast character. As elephants rule in the wild, their appearance in your dream might suggest that you reign supreme in business and at home. The number of elephants you see in a dream is significant: A herd of elephants might signify great wealth, while a single elephant might represent a small but solid life. Elephants can also symbolize memory retention, strength, and devotion.

elevator: Rising in an elevator can symbolize a raising of status, such as a promotion, or a raising of consciousness. Consider the details of the elevator ride and your feelings concerning it: Is the ascent rapid? Are you frightened? Do you feel exhilarated? A descent in an elevator might indicate a lowering in status or position, or a journey into the unconscious. Keep in mind that the dream might indicate hopes or fears rather than actual events. A stuck elevator might suggest that some aspect of your life is presently stuck. A plunging elevator could indicate a rapid descent into the unconscious.

elopement: Although dreaming of formal weddings is an omen of good fortune or happy reconciliation, dreaming of an elopement intimates that unfavorable events will occur in your life. In fact, you might lose your good reputation. And if you dream of your partner eloping with someone else, possibly you will soon learn of your partner being unfaithful.

emeralds: To dream of owning emeralds means you will inherit property. For a woman to dream of emeralds means she will soon make a smart choice in selecting a husband.

epaulets: For a man to dream of epaulets means he might be in disfavor among his friends for a time. If a woman dreams of meeting a man wearing epaulets, beware: It denotes she is about to form an unwise alliance that might end in scandal.

erotica: Erotic dreams have heightened physical sensation and are often sexually satisfying.

They can be very graphic, like an X-rated movie, and the sexual activity can be the main or only action within the dream plot. These dreams may be the mind's attempt to satisfy the natural sexual appetite, and they can be influenced by all sorts of stimuli, such as erotic novels or movies.

If you've had an erotic dream that leaves you feeling perplexed or unsettled because it's totally uncharacteristic of your true behavior in waking life, don't worry. Erotic dreams can be compared with eating rich chocolate without calories; there's no risk, no involvement, and no consequences, and hence, they are a safe place for the unconscious to play out scenarios that would never occur in real life. In other words, they fall into the category of what Freud referred to as wish fulfillment.

escaping: If you dream of making an escape, consider whether you are avoiding something in your life, or whether you need to get away from something.

Europe: If you dream of traveling to Europe, you will soon go on a long journey. This long journey will greatly increase your finances, so start packing.

evening: A dream that takes place in the evening suggests uncertain or unrealized hopes. To dream of stars shining suggests present troubles followed by brighter times. A dream of lovers walking in the evening symbolizes separation.

evergreen: A dream of an evergreen—especially the word itself—might suggest a metaphor. To be "evergreen" indicates wealth or at least financial stability. An evergreen or pine tree might also indicate hope or even immortality. A decorated evergreen or Christmas tree suggests giving or receiving gifts.

examination: Ann Faraday, in *The Dream Game*, notes that most of these dreams occur when we feel we're being "tested" or "examined" by someone, as during a job interview, for example, or perhaps in some area of our spiritual lives.

If you dream of taking an exam, it might indicate a concern about failure, or being unprepared for something. All of us feel unprepared at one time or another, and the examination dream is often a reflection of the uneasy sensation of not being ready for something coming into our lives. Pay attention to the specific elements of this sort of dream, as they will tell you more about the

An Unexpected Examination

Jim, a self-employed contractor, dreamed that he was hurrying to make an 8 A.M. class. When he got there, the professor was passing out final exam booklets. He realized that he'd been to the class only a couple of times the entire semester and that he wasn't prepared for the exam.

Although it had been more than twenty years since Jim had graduated from college, he always had this dream once or twice a year, and the specifics rarely changed. Once he began to record and study his dreams, however, he understood that the dream usually occurred when he was facing a bid on a major project. Even though he spent weeks preparing figures on a prospective project, he rarely felt adequately prepared.

scenario. For example, a stack of tests could suggest you feel you are being tested too often.

When interpreting this dream as it pertains to your own circumstances, make note of whether you're under a deadline or extreme pressure in your waking life. If you're not, then ask whether there is something in your life that you feel unprepared to cope with. (See also *missing class*.)

explosion: A dream of an explosion could be an attempt by your unconscious to get your attention to a matter of concern. An explosion could suggest a release or an outburst of repressed anger, or an upheaval in your life.

eyes: Eyes are the part of the body that allow you to see, and if you dream of them, it sometimes relates to how able you are to see certain things or situations clearly—or not. Think about your awareness of certain things in your life: Are you willing to confront things directly—with eyes wide open? Or, are you reluctant to see things for what they really are—with eyes closed?

Dreaming of eyes can also portend bad news. If you dream in color, as most people do, and you dream of brown eyes, it denotes there is deceit and treachery in your life. If you dream of blue eyes, it denotes you are weak in carrying out your intentions. Dreaming of gray eyes means you love flattery. If you dream of losing an eye or dream you have a sore eye, watch out for trouble.

F

falling: Falling is a common dream symbol and usually an expression of a concern about failure. Dreams of falling can represent a variety of metaphors, including the fallen woman, a fall from grace, or the fall season. This dream can also be a metaphor for falling down on the job, or some other role of responsibility in your life. The interpretation depends, to a large extent, on what is going on in your life at the time or what happened to you within the twenty-four hours preceding the dream. Ask yourself how you feel as you're falling: Do you feel terrified? Helpless? Out of control? Or is the sensation pleasant? If so, how?

In most falling dreams, the dreamer never lands. If you do hit the ground, it could mean that you've struck bottom in a matter. If you get up unhurt, the dream might be suggesting that you won't be hurt by something that you perceive as a failure.

fat: A dream of being fat might relate to a concern about your diet or your appearance, but it could also be a metaphor for wealth and abundance, or overindulging.

Fears Revealed in Falling

Often, a common dream theme such as falling will have an obvious "zing" to it and you'll know immediately what it's referring to. Other times, however, the dream's meaning might be as obscure as a Rubik's cube, and you'll have to take it apart piece by piece, to figure out how to put it back together. Following are two very different examples of how dreamers did just that:

After one young married woman reflected on a dream of falling from a building, it struck her as a metaphor for her affair with a married man from her office. The fall, she realized, didn't just represent a fall from grace; it was also a metaphor for what would happen to her marriage if her husband discovered the affair.

Derek, an actor, dreamed he was in a convertible with his agent, who was driving. While they were speeding along a country road, the car hit a hole and veered out of control. His agent slammed on the brakes, but the brakes failed, and they plunged over the side of a cliff. After mulling the dream over for a day or two, Derek realized that he felt as if his agent had mishandled his career and wasn't able to apply the brake to this downward spiral. He ended their partnership, and for him, the split was like a plunge over the edge of a cliff, into an abyss of the unknown.

father: The appearance of your father can have many connotations, depending on the context of the dream and your relationship with him. Typically it represents a need for advice over a troubling situation.

father-in-law: To dream of your father-in-law suggests strife with friends or a family member. To see him happy and well augurs pleasant family relations.

feather: To dream of a feather floating through the air bodes well. Your burdens will be light and easily borne. To dream of an eagle feather implies that your aspirations will be met. If a woman dreams of birds with beautiful feathers, it means she might soon find a wealthy and happy partner.

February: A dream of this short winter month suggests continued ill health and melancholy. To dream of a sunshiny day in this month may suggest an unexpected change in fortune and outlook.

fence: A dream of a fence can indicate that you feel "fenced in." A fence can block you or it can protect you. If you are "on the fence," the dream might suggest that you are undecided about something.

fever: To dream that you are suffering from a fever suggests a needless worry over a small affair.

field: To dream of green fields, ripe with corn or grain, indicates you will have great abundance. If you dream of plowed fields, you will have wealth and prestige at a young age. If you dream of a field full of dead corn, expect a dreary future.

fight: To fight in a dream might represent a conflict or the need to resolve an issue. Pay attention to other details in the dream in order to interpret it. Are you winning or losing a fight? Are you fighting with a loved one?

fire: Fire represents the power of light over darkness, and it is generally a favorable symbol to the dreamer. It often represents continued prosperity and fortune—as long as the dreamer is not burned. If you're on fire in your dream, it's probably a metaphor for passion; it's as if you are burning with desire. Fire can also symbolize a variety of other things, including wrath, destruction, purification, cleansing, illumination, and a spiritual awakening. Look at other metaphors. For instance, fire might indicate a heated situation. What are you getting "fired up" about? Are you (or another figure in the dream) concerned about "being fired" or "getting burned"?

Additionally, a dream of fire might indicate a call to gather with a community. Fire might alternatively represent the power of light over darkness.

fire engine: A symbol of distress and ultimately of protection, to dream of a fire engine indicates worry over an important matter at hand that will soon be resolved.

firefighting: To dream of fighting flames suggests that hard work is required before success in a matter at hand is achieved. To dream of a firefighter may suggest solid friendships. To dream of an injured firefighter indicates that a close friend may be in danger.

fireworks: A dream of fireworks suggests a celebration, a joyous explosion, or a release of repressed feelings.

fish: Swimming fish symbolize exploration of the unconscious or that which lies below the surface. In the Freudian interpretation, fish are phallic symbols and dreaming of fish is related to sexual desires. The Jungian interpretation theorizes that fish symbolize a spiritual quest or seeking. Other symbolic representations for fish include abundance, fertility, the potential for miracles, spirituality, spiritual forces, or a spiritual journey. Fish are sometimes even recognized as a symbol for Christ. Pay attention to the specific type of fish and its condition to glean more insight from the type of dream.

fishing: In dreams, fishing indicates a person's search for higher consciousness.

flood: Dreaming of a flood might suggest that you are being overwhelmed by a rising awareness of the unconscious aspects of your being. A dream of flooding can also serve as a warning that personal matters are spilling over into other areas of your life. Alternately, a flood can relate to a release of sexual desires or a need to do so.

flowers: Flowers in a dream can symbolize love and beauty. Flowers can also be a symbol of the inner self. New blossoms suggest the opening of the inner self. Withered and dead flowers can mean disappointment and dismal situations. To dream of a wreath of fresh flowers denotes that great opportunity will come your way. You'll have great success if you chose to take advantage of that opportunity.

flying: Dreams of flying have been subject to a variety of interpretations. Freud connected flying in a dream with the desire for sex; Alfred Adler connected these dreams with the will to dominate others; and Carl Jung saw them as the desire to break free of restrictions or inhibitions. Most psychotherapists today tend to favor Jung's interpretation. A flying dream might also suggest the dreamer is soaring, or "flying high" as a result of a successful venture.

But it's still best to look at flying dreams as individual experiences. Explore your feelings about the dream and the action that takes place. Ask yourself whether the sensation of flying is pleasurable or stressful. Why are you flying? Are you escaping pursuers? Are you showing off? Or do you feel elated? Is it merely something you're able to do? Does it seem familiar, as if you've been flying before? Also think about other specifics in these dreams, including where you go when you're flying; whether you're flying with anyone else; and whether or not you are able to choose the destination. These extra details might provide a broader context for the experience.

On another level, some people believe that dreams of flying date back to the earliest reincarnations of your soul, because they revert to a time when you had no physical form, a time when you were able to travel using the pure energy of thought as your power. In this interpretation, dreams of this sort give your soul a chance to fly again without the constraints of your physical, human body.

No matter whether the symbolic meaning is spiritual or rooted in your physical existence, flying itself can be a joyous experience in a dream.

Running to Fly

In the following dream, Ken, a forty-two-year-old insurance adjuster and an avid runner, recalled a flying dream that related to running. In a sense, it was a step beyond running.

I'm running in a field and my body is getting lighter with each stride. My steps lengthen and pretty soon I pick up speed. Then I'm airborne, I'm soaring, it's exhilarating. Then it occurs to me that I've done this before. "It's easy," I think. "Nothing to it." I tell myself I have to remember that I know how to fly.

I was excited when I woke from the dream. It took a few minutes before I realized I'd been dreaming and that I couldn't really fly in my waking life.

Ken looked at his flying dream as a symbol of accomplishment. The day of the dream he had placed second in his age bracket and twelfth overall in a local 10 kilometer race with more than seven hundred contestants. After the race, he felt elevated, and that sensation was transformed into his dream.

fog: Dreaming of foggy conditions indicates a lack of clarity in some aspect of your life. Fog can also symbolize something hidden or something you're not seeing. Keep in mind that fog is usually short-lived and when it lifts, you will gain a new sense of clarity.

forest: A forest suggests an exploration of the unconscious. It also can symbolize a need or desire to retreat from everyday life, to restore and revitalize your energies. To dream of a lush forest in complete foliage might mean prosperity and pleasure, whereas finding yourself in a dense forest can signify unpleasantness at home. A forest fire might symbolize the successful completion of your plans, with wealth and prosperity to follow.

fountain: A dream of a fountain can suggest longevity and virility. Water is related to the emotions and unconscious, so a fountain can represent an emotional surge. Alternately, a dream of a fountain might indicate an examination of your emotions. What is the condition of the fountain? A clear fountain suggests vast possessions and many pleasures. A dry and broken fountain symbolizes the end of pleasure. A sparkling fountain in the moonlight can indicate an ill-advised pleasure.

fox: A fox symbolizes cunning, charm, and craftiness when it's most needed.

friends: If you dream of a gathering of your friends and they are all happy, you will have a pleasant event to attend soon. If you dream of a gathering of your friends and they are sad and gloomy, call them, because something is probably amiss.

frog: Frogs, like the prince who was turned into one, are transformative creatures. They start as tadpoles, grow legs and arms, and develop lungs. To dream of a frog may imply a major change or transformation in your life. Since frogs live part of their lives in water, a frog might also symbolize a leap into the unconscious. They also represent renewal, particularly in health-related matters.

frost: Frost, like ice, may represent an emotional state of the dreamer or a person in the dream. To see a friend or lover in frost could mean chilly feelings regarding the relationship.

gale: If, of all things, you dream you are caught in a gale, watch out—you might have business losses.

gambling: Dreaming of gambling suggests taking a chance. If you are winning, it might bode well for a risky business deal. If you're watching others win, the game might symbolize a fear of taking a chance. Whether you should be more daring or play it safe depends on other factors in the dream.

garbage: To dream of garbage suggests a need to get rid of old, worn-out ideas, or excess baggage in your life. Ask yourself if you are clinging to something or some condition that you no longer need.

garden: A garden sometimes indicates a need to bring more beauty into your life. It might be a metaphor for personal or spiritual growth, or a desire to cultivate a new talent or move into a higher realm of awareness. If you dream of a garden, consider its upkeep, and this will give you insight into the meaning. A flourishing garden suggests good health, while a garden with lots of weeds might symbolize a need to weed out old, outmoded ideas or a desire to cultivate your spiritual self.

gardening: A dream that involves gardening portends a coming surprise.

garret: Dreaming of the top of a house—a garret—indicates that good times are coming your way. If you dream you are climbing stairs to a garret, that dream is telling you that you tend to dwell in theories of life and leave the everyday realities to others. Perhaps you should think about changing your ways.

gate: A gate might represent a portal from one state of being to another. Is there a gatekeeper? Do you meet the gatekeeper's criteria for passage to the next level? (See also *door.*)

ghost: An apparition or ghost appearing in a dream might suggest that something in your life is elusive or out of reach. If a person who has died appears in a dream, consider your past relationship to that person and what that individual symbolized in your life. A ghost of a living relative or friend in a dream might symbolize that you are in danger from someone you know, or if that ghost appears haggard it might signify an early death or a breaking off of a friendship.

giraffe: Dreaming of a giraffe implies stretching yourself or being more open-minded.

giving birth: Dreaming of being in labor or giving birth does not have to signify the literal birth of a baby. Often, these dreams occur when beginning something new, or diving into a creative task. Giving birth can represent anything from taking on a new project at work, to starting a new hobby, such as painting or writing. (See also *birth*.)

glass: Glass is suggestive of separation and passive observation. Looking through glass in a dream can symbolize bitter disappointment clouding your brightest hopes. Receiving cut glass in a dream may suggest a reward for your efforts.

gloves: If you dream you are wearing gloves, regardless of the weather, it's a signal that you should exercise caution in your financial dealings. To dream of old, ragged gloves signifies you might possibly suffer a loss or, worse, be betrayed. But to dream of finding a pair of gloves can mean a marriage is on your horizon, or that you will start a new love affair. This is good news if you are single; it can, however, complicate your life if you are married.

God image: If you dream of some sort of image or representation of God, this is usually an indication of good health.

goblet: A goblet is yet another strong feminine symbol of the womb and the Goddess. Additionally, drinking from one cup is a Wiccan and Pagan symbol of unity.

gold: Dreaming of gold jewelry or coins or a gold object indicates that success is forthcoming. The color gold, when it appears in dreams, signifies good health.

goose: Since a goose is often associated with a golden egg, it's not surprising that dreaming of one is a symbol of abundance. On the other hand, a goose in the oven or on fire suggests "your goose is cooked." Alternately, a "big goose egg" can mean zero or nothing. One other interpretation is that good news is forthcoming, possibly combined with improved communication skills and creative aptitude.

grandparents: Your own attitude about your grandparents will provide you with the most clues regarding the meaning of this dream. However, in general, grandparents represent the accrued wisdom that comes with age, and they also conjure a feeling of being safe, protected, and loved unconditionally.

grass: To dream of green grass signifies good things will happen in your life. If you are in business, you will soon be wealthy. If you are an artist, you soon will become well known. If you are about to marry, you will have a safe, happy life with your partner.

grave: Like many dream symbols, a grave is one that grabs your attention, especially if it's your grave. A grave can portend a death, but not necessarily a physical one. It might mean that you're leaving the old behind, moving on to something new, as in experiencing a transition. As a metaphor, a grave also suggests that you might be dealing with a grave matter. (See also *death*.)

green: When green is a dominant color in a dream, it can be interpreted symbolically, like any object in a dream. Green is a color of healing and good health, of growth, of money, and of new beginnings. It suggests positive movement in a matter at hand.

gun: A gun in your possession can symbolize protection, but it is also a phallic symbol and a sign of aggressive male behavior. If you shoot yourself, the act is what's important, not the gun. (See also *suicide*.)

gypsy: The typical notion of gypsies is that they never stay rooted in one place, and in dreams, they might imply wandering, restlessness, and movement. If you encounter a gypsy in your dreams, it might also be an indication of unexpressed psychic potential.

hail: To dream of being in a hailstorm, or to hear hail hitting against the house, represents being besieged by a troubling matter, thoughts, or emotions. However, if you dream of watching hail fall through sunshine and rain, it might suggest that fortune and pleasure will shine on you after a brief period of trouble or misery.

hair: Hair can appear in many different ways and is open to many interpretations. To dream that you have a beautiful head of hair and are combing it indicates thoughts of appearance over substance. To see your hair turn unexpectedly white suggests sudden misfortune and grief over a situation at hand, while a dream that you have a full head of white hair suggests a pleasing and fortunate passage through life. For a man to dream that his hair is thinning suggests misfortune due to generosity, or illness through worry. To see yourself covered in hair represents an indulgence in vice, while a dream of tangled and unkempt hair suggests trouble or concern over a matter at hand. For a woman to compare a white hair with a black one taken from her head symbolizes a hesitation between two paths.

hammer: A hammer might suggest strength or power. However, because it can be used for either constructive or destructive purposes, how the hammer is used is the key to its meaning.

hand: A dream about a hand (or hands) is open to numerous interpretations, depending on what the hand (or hands) is doing and the surrounding circumstances. Shaking hands represents an act of friendship or an agreement. Hands folded in prayer might suggest you are seeking help or pursuing religious or spiritual urgings. A hand that is grasping at something might indicate a fear of death. As a metaphor, a hand can suggest that something important is "at hand." To see beautiful hands in a dream signifies feelings of great honor and rapid advancement in a matter at hand. Ugly and malformed hands point to disappointment and poverty. A detached hand represents solitude; people might fail to understand your views and feeling in a matter. Burning your hands in a dream suggests that you have overreached your abilities and will suffer some loss because of it. A dream of washing your hands indicates participation in some joyous affair.

handkerchiefs: Most people don't carry cloth handkerchiefs today, availing themselves of tissues instead, but if you should dream of a handkerchief, it means you will embark on a flirtatious affair. That's good news if you are single. If you dream of losing a handkerchief, it indicates a broken engagement will possibly occur. A torn handkerchief portends you will have a lovers' quarrel, and a reconciliation will be impossible. To dream of silk handkerchiefs is much better. It denotes that your pleasing and magnetic personality will make an auspicious existence for yourself.

happiness: Don't read too much into this one. To dream of happiness, quite simply, means happy events will occur in your life.

harming others: If in a dream you harm others, through deceit, telling lies, or injuring their reputation in some way, it indicates that your own reputation is about to plummet.

harvest: A harvest represents completion and abundance, and might indicate that your reward is due. As with all symbols, personal connotations are important. For instance, if you grew up on a farm, the dream could mean a longing to return to the past or to simpler times.

hat: A hat covers the head and can suggest that the person wearing it is concealing something, as in "keep it under your hat." Dreaming that you have a feather in your hat indicates achievement.

hawk: A hawk is a creature with keen sight. A soaring hawk in a dream might suggest the need for insight. It also might mean that the dreamer should keep a "hawk's eye" on a certain someone or situation.

head: Dreaming of a human head could indicate that you are ahead, or successful, on a matter of importance. A head also symbolizes a source of wisdom.

healer: Dreaming of a healing figure is generally indicative of good health.

hearing voices: Dreaming that you are hearing pleasant voices indicates joyous reconciliations will happen in your future. If the voices are angry, expect disappointments; if the voices are weeping, expect to have a sudden outburst of anger.

If you hear the voice of God, honorable people will soon praise you for your unselfishness and generosity.

heart: To see a heart might relate to romantic inclinations. Is there a "heart throb" in your life? Alternately, the image might suggest you get to the "heart of the matter." On the negative side, if your heart is bleeding, it could mean that excessive sympathy is becoming a burden for you or the recipient, or both.

heel: The heel of your foot or shoe can symbolize vulnerability, as in the Achilles' heel story. It might also stand for an oppressive situation, as in "under someone's heel." Are you dealing with someone who is not trustworthy? He or she could be the heel in question.

hell: Beware if hell is a central element in a dream. If in your dream you are actually in hell with the devil, this indicates that you are in danger of falling into temptations that could destroy you and your reputation. If you dream of friends being trapped in hell, you will soon hear of your friends' misfortunes.

helmet: Wearing a helmet in a dream denotes protection. The helmet could also symbolize that you need to guard your time, thoughts, or ideas.

hen: To dream of hens means you will attend a pleasant family reunion.

herbs: To dream of herbs means there will soon be pleasure in your life. However, dreaming of poisonous herbs indicates your enemies are gossiping about you. A dream about useful herbs means satisfaction in business and also suggests that warm friendships will soon be yours.

hero: A familiar archetypal symbol, heroes are strong, courageous, and capable. Heroes step up to the greatest of challenges, and they continue their quests, struggles, and battles, even when the odds seem stacked against them. According to Layne Dalfen in *Dreams Do Come True,* "Hero images can arise in a dream during times of transition, when you need the courage to look deeper inside yourself for some answers.

And while that idea might be frightening, it is the hero in you who will forge ahead despite any fear you might be facing." Therefore, dreaming of a hero can encourage you to believe that you, too, have the ability to call on your own inner strength—strength that initially you might not have even recognized you had.

high tide: To dream of a high tide symbolizes that a change, usually favorable, is in order, as in the phrase the "tides are turning."

hogs: A fat hog in a dream might suggest abundance, while a lean, hungry hog could foretell of a troubling situation. If you grew up on a farm with hogs, the dream could relate to some aspect of your childhood. If the hogs are wallowing in mud, the indication might be that you've lowered your standards regarding a matter, or that you are groveling. The dream could also be a warning of such possibilities. A squealing hog suggests that something distasteful has occurred or will soon occur.

horoscope: If you dream your astrological chart is being cast, you will have unexpected changes in your life (you probably will be taking a long journey). You also will be dealing with strangers regarding your business affairs. If you dream a soothsayer is reading the stars and predicting your future, you will probably find disappointment in life.

horse: A horse symbolizes strength, power, endurance, majesty, and virility. A man dreaming of a horse might desire virility and sexual prowess; a woman might be expressing a desire for sexual intercourse. Riding a horse suggests one is in a powerful position. White horses represent purity, while black horses represent a postponement of pleasure. Horses are also significant as symbols of movement/travel, transitions, messages, or ambitions.

hospital: Finding oneself in a hospital suggests a need for healing, or a concern about one's health. Seeing someone else in a hospital might indicate that person is in a weakened condition. If you work in a hospital, the meaning of the dream could relate to work matters. In the latter case, other circumstances in the dream should be examined.

house: Houses are common forums for dreams, and are sometimes thought to represent the body or the self. They might, however, be of little consequence unless the house itself is the focus of the dream. If so, examine the type of house and its size. Discovering new rooms in a house or following secret passages in an old house can relate to an exploration of the unconscious. A small house might suggest a feeling of confinement. If a house is under construction, it could symbolize growth. If it's dilapidated, it suggests improvements are needed in some part of the dreamer's life.

hugging: To dream you are hugging a stranger suggests that you crave affection. If you know the person you are hugging, the interpretation will depend on your relationship to that person.

humidity: Dreaming of humidity represents the presence of an oppressive situation, either in work or at home.

hummingbird: A dream that includes a hummingbird suggests a blast from the past (possibly a former lover) is about to appear.

hurricane: Destructive and unpredictable, dreaming of a hurricane can suggest different meanings depending on their context in the dream. To hear and see a hurricane coming at you symbolizes a feeling of torture and suspense regarding a matter in which you are trying to avert failure. To dream of looking at the debris of a hurricane suggests that you will come close to calamity, but will be saved by the efforts of others. A dream in which you are in a house that is shattered by a hurricane and you are trying to save someone caught in the rubble might represent that your life will suffer many changes but that there is still no peace in domestic or business matters. To see people dead and wounded suggests that you are concerned over the troubles of others.

husband: The husband-wife relationship is the primary bond in life; thus, to dream of your husband usually arises out of issues related to the joys and troubles of everyday life. The general atmosphere of the dream often speaks to whether it's positive or negative. If positive images or events are involved in your dream of your husband, it probably bodes well. However, if negative events or images are involved, it might be signifying your own fears or concerns. (Although this does not necessarily mean they are true-to-life fact.) (See also *wife*.)

ice: Ice can symbolize an emotional state of the dreamer or a person in the dream. Are you receiving an "icy reception"? If you are in a tenuous situation, you could be "skating on thin ice." In a sexual context, ice represents frigidity. To dream of ice floating in a clear stream signifies an interruption of happiness, while dreaming of eating ice portends sickness.

ice cream: A dream of ice cream, especially melting ice cream, might suggest that obstacles are being removed and that there is reason to celebrate. If ice cream is your favorite dessert, then the dream suggests that you're being rewarded or have reason to treat yourself. It can also stand for a desire for sexual fulfillment.

icicles: Icicles represent danger or your concern over a matter that is hanging over you in some way. To dream of icicles falling off of trees or the eaves of a house may suggest that some misfortune will soon disappear. To dream of icicles on evergreens symbolizes that a bright future may be overshadowed by doubt.

illness: If you dream of being ill, ask yourself if you're in need of being cared for and pampered. This dream might also be a message to watch your health.

incense: Incense is often used in holy rituals and, therefore, it can represent prayers or requests being directed to a Spirit. Incense alternatively represents cleansing and life as a ritual.

incest: A dream of a sexual encounter with someone within your family is not necessarily a warning about incest. Examine your relationship with the person in question. If there have been arguments or you're alienated from this family member, the dream might be your inner self expressing your love in a shocking way that will catch your attention.

infants: Seeing infants in a dream suggests that pleasant surprises are near. Seeing an infant swimming represents a fortunate escape from some endeavor.

inheritance: Dreaming you come into an inheritance naturally indicates good things will happen in your life. In fact, dreaming of inheriting money denotes that you will be successful and you will achieve your dreams quite easily.

initiation: Initiation suggests that a new path is opening for you. It could be a career change or advancement. Often, initiatory dreams also relate to a spiritual quest.

insects: In general, insects represent small aggravations or things that are "bugging" you. Specific meanings can change dramatically depending on which type of insect appears as well as the overall context of the dream. For example, if you dream of ants, you might be feeling "antsy" about a particular matter. (See also *ant.*)

interview: Being interviewed in a dream is similar to taking an examination. It suggests you're being judged. If you're surprised by the interview, it could indicate that you are feeling unprepared.

invalid: A dream of an invalid might indicate that you (or someone else) feel weak or incapable of living independently.

invocation: If an invocation is involved in your dream, it indicates the call of your soul to the Divine for assistance or presence.

iris: Irises predict forthcoming communications from friends or loved ones.

island: An island can be viewed as an exotic place or as a separate, isolated land. Dreaming of an island might mean that a vacation is due, especially if "going to the islands" is a vacation destination. Alternately, finding yourself on an "desert island" might suggest you are cut off from others or from your inner self.

ivy: Dreaming of ivy growing on trees or a house indicates you will have excellent health and success. Many joys in your life could follow this dream. For a young woman, dreaming of ivy clinging to a wall in moonlight portends she will have a secret affair with a young man. Beware of dreaming of withered ivy. It indicates broken engagements and sadness.

jail: In a dream, a jail might indicate that you're feeling restricted or confined and fear being punished. Or you might believe that you should be punished. Dreaming of being a jailer suggests the desire to control others or to gain more control of your own life.

January: To dream of this month might mean that you will be associated with unloved companions or children.

jaws: Do you feel like you're under attack? Jaws can be the entry point to an archetypal journey into the underworld. Such a dream might also relate to a disagreement.

jet: Dreaming of the stone jet warns of sadness ahead.

jewelry: In a material sense, jewelry can symbolize affluence, but look to other aspects of the dream for confirmation. Jewelry can also stand for inner wealth, psychic protection, or healing.

jewels: Precious gems make the best gifts, and dreaming of jewels, in general, signifies good luck to come.

job: Dreaming that you are at work on the job might indicate that you're overworked, you're deeply focused on some aspect of your job, or you desire to work harder and achieve more.

joy: Dreaming of joy—a feeling of well-being and good fortune—means that there will be harmony among all your friends.

judge: If you're the judge, the dream suggests that you have a choice to make. A judge can also represent justice or fairness. Alternately, a judge might stand for a part of you that criticizes your impulsive behavior. Or perhaps you're concerned that you are being judged. If so, think about who it is that's judging you.

July: A dream that takes place in this month symbolizes a depressed outlook that will suddenly change to unimagined pleasure and good fortune.

jumping: Pick your metaphor: Are you "a jump ahead," "jumping to conclusions," "jumping the gun," or "jumping for joy"? A series of jumps might be the take-off point for a flying dream. A great leap can also symbolize success or achievement or "a leap of faith."

June: A dream that takes place in June symbolizes unusual gains in all undertakings. For a woman to dream of vegetation, dying, or a drought during this month suggests a lasting sorrow and loss.

jungle: A jungle might represent a hidden, dark part of the self that you've been avoiding. Your unconscious might be telling you of a need to explore this part of yourself. It could also represent a great, untapped fertility for spiritual growth within you.

junk: If you dream of junk or clutter, ask yourself if you're clinging to the past, to things or ideas that are no longer useful. If something you value appears as junk in a dream, it may indicate that you need to reassess your values.

kangaroo: To see a kangaroo might suggest the dreamer is "hopping mad" about something. It could also mean that you have the ability to "hop to" a particular matter that is pending.

key: Keys represent entrance: They open doors, start cars, and allow us to get inside of our homes and offices. If you dream of losing keys, this signifies that you are being denied entrance or access to somewhere or something. If, on the other hand, you recover your keys in a dream, it indicates that you are regaining that access.

A key can also stand for a part of yourself that you've locked away, and in that case, the same notions of losing or retrieving a key would apply, just directly to yourself. A dream of this sort might also indicate you hold the key to your own concerns.

killing: A dream of killing someone is probably not a warning that you might turn into a killer. Instead, the meaning is more likely a symbolic act of aggression. Whom did you kill and how is that person involved in your life? If you don't recognize the person, the dream might symbolize killing off an unwanted part of yourself.

king: A king is a ruler and a powerful authority figure. Dreaming of a king might mean you are seeking status or support. The king might represent your father or some other powerful figure in your life. If you're the king, the indication is that you have achieved a high level of authority or are a highly capable individual.

kiss: A kiss suggests a romantic involvement, but it can also be a metaphor as in "kiss and make up," or the "kiss of death." In the former, the dream kiss might indicate a reconciliation is at hand. A kiss of death spells the end to something, such as a way of life. For married people to kiss each other symbolizes harmony in the home life. Is it dark or light out during the kiss? The former suggests danger or an illicit situation while the latter represents honorable intentions. To dream of kissing someone on the neck symbolizes a passionate inclination in a matter at hand.

kitchen: Going to a kitchen in a dream suggests some part of your life is in need of nourishment. Alternatively, a kitchen might suggest that something is in the process of being "cooked up," like a new project. Note what you're doing in the kitchen.

kitten: To discover kittens in a closet or a basement suggests the awakening of hidden aspects of the self. It can also relate to new ideas and projects. (See also *cat*.)

kneeling: In basic terms, kneeling is equivalent to not standing up. By association, when you're not standing, you can't walk, advance, or move forward well. Not surprisingly, then, a dream in which you're kneeling could have ties to all of these things. Consider whether there is something or someone in your life holding you back, or someone or something you can't "stand up to." Kneeling also puts you at a different level than one who is standing, so consider whether or not you feel as if you don't have "equal ground" on something.

On another level, kneeling is a common sign of reverence and prayer. Therefore, it can also relate to feelings of God's power and authority and, by extension, the power and authority of anyone else who is important in your life—a parent, for example, who represents authority to you in your life. In this case, consider whether you might be blowing that sense of authority out of proportion, if it makes you feel subjugated to the point of kneeling before that person.

knife: A knife is a symbol of aggression and the male sexual organ. Examine the other aspects of the dream. Are you being stabbed in the back? Do you hold the knife or is someone threatening you with it? A rusty knife might symbolize dissatisfaction, a sharp knife worry, and a broken knife defeat.

knight: A knight signifies honor and high standing. Are you searching for a knight or are you acting like a knight? Knights are also armored and stand for protection.

knob: A knob appearing in a dream might imply a need to get a handle on a matter. Knobs also signify a means of passing from one room to the next, or one way of life to another.

knot: Knots tie things together and in dreams they can signify the binding of negative or unwanted energy—or holding energy in place until it's needed. Dreaming of knots also suggests

that you might be "all tied up" about something—
that worries or anxieties are troubling you. You
might feel as if you're "tied in a knot." Alternately,
if you or someone close to you is "tying the
knot," the dream might signify a concern about
an upcoming marriage.

laboratory: A laboratory is a place where experiments are conducted. The implication is that the dreamer is unsatisfied with a present situation and experimenting with something new. The dreamer might also be testing a relationship with someone.

labyrinth: Labyrinths are full of twists and turns, and as such, are a symbol of being lost and confused. A dream of a labyrinth or maze might indicate that you feel trapped in a situation or a relationship and are looking for a way out. It might also refer to the intricacies of a spiritual journey. (See also *maze*.)

lace: Overall, to dream of lace denotes good times ahead. For a man to dream of his lover wearing lace means two good things will happen. He will have her faithfulness in love, and he will probably get a job promotion. For a woman to dream of wearing lace denotes happiness, and if she dreams of making lace, that indicates she will meet a good-looking and wealthy man who will propose. She supposedly will also reach her ambitions and her lover will fulfill her every wish. If you dream of buying lace, you will have wealth. Watch out when you dream you are selling lace—your ambitions will outrun your resources.

ladder: Are you going up or climbing down the ladder? An ascent might symbolize a higher step into an inner realm or a promotion to a higher status in one's career or other pursuits.

lagoon: Lagoons symbolize doubt and confusion over an emotional matter or a stagnant situation.

lake: In the Freudian interpretation, a lake is symbolic of the vagina. In the Jungian world, lakes and other bodies of water stand for the unconscious or emotions. In one interpretation, the dreamer who dives into a lake is returning to the womb. In the other, the dreamer explores the unconscious. But if neither interpretation fits, examine the other elements in the dream. Is the lake clear? This could suggest lucidity and strength of purpose; if the water is tranquil and you can see your reflection, might this imply that you are reflecting—or need to reflect on—certain things in your life? If the water is muddy, it might represent muddled feelings and an unsure direction in a matter at hand.

lamb: A lamb might stand for gentleness or vulnerability, as in "a lamb to the slaughter," or it may be a spiritual symbol as in "sacrificial lamb" and "lamb of God." However, a dream of a lamb might simply symbolize a general love of animals.

lamp: A lamp, like a lantern, represents light or illumination and suggests the dreamer is searching for truth.

lap: A symbol of security, such as "the lap of luxury," to dream of sitting on someone's lap signifies safety from some troubling situation. A dream of a cat in a lap represents danger from a seductive enemy.

lapis: Dreaming of the stone lapis suggests that magickal awareness is growing in or around you.

lawsuits: Dreams of legal matters suggest the dreamer is being judged.

leeches: Leeches are nightmarish creatures that suck blood. If you dream of leeches, consider if there is some person or situation in your life that is draining your energy. Leeches can also symbolize difficult transitions. (See also *death*.)

legs: Legs in various states of health and appearance are frequently seen in dreams and open to many interpretations depending on the context. To dream of admiring well-shaped legs suggests a loss of judgment; to see misshapen legs represents unsuccessful endeavors and ill-tempered friends. A wooden leg represents deception to friends, while a wounded leg suggests a loss of power and standing. A dream of ulcers on your legs suggests a drain on your resources to help others. A young woman who admires her own legs indicates vanity, and if she has hairy legs then it may indicate feelings of domination over her mate. Dreaming that your own legs are clean and well shaped represents a happy future with faithful friends.

leopard: If you dream of a leopard attacking you, you might encounter many difficulties working toward future success. But if you kill the leopard, you will be victorious in life. Dreaming of a caged leopard means that although your enemies surround you, they will fail to injure you.

letter: A letter sometimes symbolizes a message from your unconscious to you. If you're unable to read the letter, look at other aspects of the dream for clues. An anonymous letter could signify an injurious concern from an unspecified source. Blue ink symbolizes steadfastness and affection, red ink suggests suspicion and jealousy, and a letter with a black border possibly represent distress and death of some kind. Receiving a letter written on black paper with white ink might suggest feelings of misery and disappointment over a matter. If this letter passed between husband and wife or lovers, then concerns over the relationship might be present. A torn letter might suggest concerns that hopeless mistakes could ruin your reputation.

lightning: A dream of lightning indicates a flash of inspiration or sudden awareness about the truth of a matter. Lightning can also mean a purging or purification, or fear of authority or death.

lion: To dream of a lion signifies that you are driven by a great force. Subduing a lion indicates victory in a matter. If you are overtaken by the lion, the dream suggests that you might be vulnerable to an attack of some sort. A caged lion might mean that you will succeed as long as the opposition to your goal is held in check. Lions also represent authority, protection, and ferocity when necessary to defend something you love.

lizard: Since lizards shed their skin, it stands to reason that dreaming of one suggests the ability to break away from the old and begin anew.

lodestone: Because it is known for its magnetic (attractive) qualities, lodestone represents something that will approach you.

lottery: To dream of a lottery signifies chance or throwing your fate to luck. If you dream of holding the winning number, then luck and good fortune in a matter at hand may follow. To see others winning in a lottery could suggest that many friends will be brought together in a pleasing manner. A young woman dreaming of a lottery might indicate a reckless attitude.

luggage: Luggage stands for your personal effects or what you carry with you on a journey. What happens to the luggage in your dream? Lost luggage might be a concern about your identity or about being prepared for the journey. Stolen luggage might suggest that you feel someone is interfering with your attempt to reach a goal.

magic: In dreams, the presence of magic represents personal power that requires responsibility and control. In another sense, magick could point to the magical aspects of creativity or, on the darker side, to deceit and trickery.

malachite: If you dream of malachite, this suggests you will soon find a peaceful resolution to a problem or disagreement.

man: To dream of a handsome man, some individual you do not know, represents an enjoyment of life. If the man is disfigured, then perplexities and sorrow might involve you in a matter at hand. For a woman to dream of a handsome man can suggest that distinction will be offered.

manuscript: A manuscript represents the collection of your hopes and desires. To interpret the dream, note the shape or appearance of the manuscript. Is it finished or unfinished? Are you at work on it? Did you lose it?

map: You're searching for a new path to follow or are being guided in a new direction.

March: A dream that occurs in this month may symbolize unsatisfactory results in a business matter.

mask: Masks hide our appearances and our feelings from others, but the dream could also indicate that you are hiding your emotions on a particular matter from yourself. If others are wearing masks, then perhaps you are confronted with a situation in which you think someone is not being truthful.

May: A dream of May indicates fortunate times and pleasures for the young. To dream of a freakish appearance of nature suggests sudden sorrow and misery.

maze: Mazes are full of twists and turns and as such, they often represent a complicated situation that you can't find your way out of. (See also *labyrinth.*)

medicine: Taking medicine in a dream can be a potent symbol of healing your "wounds." It also suggests that you have "to take your medicine," and do what is necessary or required of you.

merriment: To dream of being merry, full of gaiety and high spirits, means that pleasant events and affairs will soon prove profitable.

merry-go-round: A merry-go-round suggests that you are going round and round in life and not moving ahead. The same would apply to someone else you dream of on a merry-go-round.

meteor: A meteor or falling star might symbolize that your wish will come true, or it could suggest that you are engaged in wishful thinking. Look at the other elements in the dream and decide which possibility is true for you.

microphone: A microphone might symbolize the desire to draw attention to yourself, or to gain power over others. Alternately, a microphone could suggest a concern that you are not forceful enough, and need help in projecting yourself.

microscope: A microscope symbolizes the need or wish to find something that's out of sight or hidden from you.

milk: Milk symbolizes nurturing. It can also represent strength and virility. To dream of milk portends prosperity and happiness. For a farmer dreaming of milk, it could mean an abundant harvest. For the traveler, it means an important and successful voyage. For women to dream of milk means they will possibly be prosperous.

To see large quantities of milk in your dreams means you will be rich and healthy. If you dream of giving milk away, it suggests you are too generous for your own good and your own fortune. Dreaming of sour milk means you will be upset over a friend's distress.

mirror: Reflection is the primary metaphor that comes to mind when thinking of a mirror. This representation can play out in diverse ways, including reflecting energy in one direction or another, or suggesting the need to reconsider your self-image.

missing class: Like dreams of examinations, if in your dream you forgot to go to a class, this might suggest that you are worried about being unprepared. (See also *examination*.)

mist: Like fog, mist indicates a period of temporary uncertainty. Seeing others in a mist may mean that you will profit by their misfortune and uncertainty.

mistletoe: To dream of mistletoe signifies great happiness and honor is to come your way. If you are young and dream of mistletoe, it indicates you will have many pleasant times in your future.

money: Money represents energy, power, and influence. Dreaming of gaining money suggests abundance; losing sums of money symbolizes a draining of energy, power, and influence. To dream of stealing money suggests danger.

money tree: The old adage that "Money doesn't grow on trees" is one that is often engrained in many of us from the time we're children. It's no surprise, then, that money trees often show up in dreams as metaphors. If you dream of finding money or coins in the ground, growing in the roots of a tree, think about how roots are the hidden strength of a tree—without them the tree dies. Then, consider how this symbol of hidden strength might apply to various aspects of your life (the connection need not be a strictly literal connection to wealth or finances). If in your dream you find yourself digging deeper, and you continue to find more and more coins, this is usually symbolic of digging within yourself. The inner self roots us to our true nature, and therein lies an abundance of riches, which are often greater than we realize.

monkey: Monkeys symbolize playfulness or flattery—and not always with good results.

moon: If you dream of the moon, and especially if it is the predominant feature, this could imply the development of your intuitive senses. Once believed to be the source of a witch's power, the phase of the moon changes the meaning of this symbol in your dreams. A full moon, for example, would indicate coming into full awareness of potential, whereas a waning moon might indicate that inner resources are wanting.

The moon is also a source of illumination and might symbolize light reflecting in the dark if there is a situation or issue occurring in your life that you feel is in need of direction or clarity. (See also *cat* and *owl*.)

moonstone: A dream that includes the gem moonstone speaks of improved foresight.

morning: Morning represents a fresh start, or a sudden change of fortune for the positive. To dream of a cloudy morning indicates that heavy matters may overwhelm you.

mother: To see your mother symbolizes pleasing results from any endeavor. What is the context in which she appears? To converse with her suggests you might soon receive good news.

Dreaming of Relatives

In general, dreams of parents—or even siblings, grandparents, and other family members, for that matter—can reflect an element of authority, responsibility, or accountability, especially if you admire certain qualities in or value the opinions of these individuals. Think about the specific qualities of the person you're dreaming about, and consider whether these are traits to which you're aspiring at present. Or, if the family figures in your dreams are critical and disapproving of you in your dream, consider what they might be judging, what their judgments mean to you, and whether or not the dream elucidates what your best interest in a situation might be. On the other hand, if you are overly concerned in your dream about your family's approval and judgments, then this might point to issues regarding your perceived fear of the authority or control they have on you. Perhaps in your real life it's time to take a stand on your own thoughts and decisions and make your feelings known to the people you love.

Keep in mind that just because you dream of a particular relative, that doesn't mean that all the implications relate to that person. One family member can represent another in dreams, or even stand for the concept of your family as a whole. They can also reflect—or even contradict—elements of yourself.

To hear your mother calling represents that you are in need of a correction in your life.

mother-in-law: A dream in which your mother-in-law appears suggests that a pleasant reconciliation is in order over a matter after some serious disagreement.

mountain: A mountain represents a challenge. If you're climbing the mountain, you're working to achieve your goals. Descending a mountain suggests that things are easier now; your success might have ensured your future.

mouse: A dream that includes a mouse indicates frugality through innovation.

mud: Mud represents the need for cleansing or purification in dreams. (See also *weeds*).

mule: Mules are known for their contrary behavior, as in "stubborn as a mule." To dream of a mule suggests that the dreamer might be acting in a stubborn manner that others find annoying. Mules also are work animals. Consider whether you are rebelling against some aspect of your job or career.

murder: Murder symbolizes repressed anger, either at yourself or others. If you murder someone you know, consider your relationship with that person. If you're the one murdered, then the dream may symbolize a personal transformation.

music: Music in a dream symbolizes emotional matters. Consider the type of music you heard and how you related to it. Did it fill you with joy? Did it make you sad or angry?

nail: A nail in a dream can have a variety of meanings, so consider the context. For example, to "nail it down" suggests putting something together or holding it together. Or, if you "hit the nail on the head," you've gotten something exactly right, articulated something perfectly, and so on.

naked/nudity: The first reaction to such a dream might be to consider its practical implications. If, for instance, you are about to embark on a trip and dreamed of being naked while traveling, check your luggage to make sure you're taking everything you need.

But like other common dreams, the nudity is more likely symbolic. Finding oneself naked in a public place, such as on a busy street, is embarrassing. If you've had such an experience, you probably were relieved when you realized that it was a dream. Being nude in a dream points to a feeling of being exposed or vulnerable—remember, exposure can be good or bad. This type of dream could mean you're exposed to the criticism of others, but it might also symbolize a wish for exposure, as in a desire to be seen or heard. Are you looking for exposure, for example, to publicize something you've done? In a case like that, the dream might even suggest that the exposure that you've been seeking is about to occur.

A dream of being naked can also relate to a need to bare the truth—or hide it. Think about whether or not you are hiding something that you've done from the public view. In either case, a nudity dream brings to light a concern.

A "naked" dream can also be a desire dream, depending on how you perceive your nakedness in the dream. If people have a positive reaction to you, for example, and you also enjoy and/or revel in your exhibitionism in the dream, it means that your wish is to expose yourself, to make yourself vulnerable to others. This is a good sign, and a healthy one.

Alternately, this type of dream can be sexually related and suggests that the dreamer is no longer inhibited. To dream of swimming naked might represent an illicit affair that will end badly, or that you have many admirers.

neck: A neck can be a sexual symbol related to the slang term necking. A neck can also represent taking a chance, as in "sticking your neck out." Alternately, if there is pain related to this part of the body, something might be giving you a "pain in the neck."

needle: A dream of a needle and thread might indicate that a matter is being sewn up, or a deal is being completed. A needle might also suggest that someone is needling you. To dream of threading a needle symbolizes that you might be burdened with caring for others; to look for a needle augurs useless worries. To break a needle in a dream signifies loneliness and poverty.

neighbor: If you dream of a neighbor, be prepared to spend hours ironing out problems due to unwarranted gossip. If you dream your neighbor is sad—watch out. You might quarrel with that neighbor.

nest: A nest is a symbol of home and might relate to the desire to return home. If you are moving, it might relate to your concerns about your new home. If there is an egg in the nest, the dream might pertain to a concern about your savings or "nest egg."

night: A night setting for a dream might suggest something is hidden or obscured, and there might be a need to illuminate something in your life. Being surrounded by night in a dream suggests oppression and hardship.

nightingale: If you dream you are sitting in a garden listening to the song of a nightingale, you will be prosperous, healthy, and happy.

nose: A nose can be a symbol of intrusive behavior, as in "sticking your nose into someone else's business." Dreaming of a nose might suggest that someone else is interfering in your life, or that you are the one who's being nosy.

November: November dreams usually suggest a season of indifferent success in all affairs.

numbers: As with dreams of people who are a certain age, numbers in dreams can relate to various aspects of your life, from the number of the street address where you live or work, to the age of a family member or friend, to a significant day of the month, date, or year for you. Don't neglect to break the numbers down using addition, subtraction, multiplication, or division, in order to dig for various other implications for the numbers. (See also *age*.)

nurse: A dream of a nurse suggests that you are being healed or are in need of healing. It also implies a desire to be pampered or nursed. Nurses provide assistance also; consider, therefore, if you are unconsciously in need of or seeking assistance with something happening in your waking life.

The dream could also relate to a relationship or a project that you are "nursing" along. (See also *doctor* and *physician*.)

nursing: A dream of nursing could indicate an idea or situation that needs nurturing.

oak tree: An oak tree represents strength, stability, endurance, truth, and wisdom. A dream with an oak might suggest that a strong, proper foundation has been established in a matter. To dream of a mighty oak can also portend success. Dreaming of a forest of oak trees signifies you will have prosperity in all aspects of your life.

oar: An oar can represent masculinity and strength; it dips into the water, the emotions. To row vigorously suggests a need for aggressiveness or that you are moving through an issue. If in your dream you have only one oar and are rowing in a circle, it might suggest frustration at the lack of forward movement.

oasis: An oasis suggests that you've arrived at a place of sustenance, that you are being nurtured. Or it might suggest that you're taking a break from your journey or have succeeded in reaching one destination on the journey. Alternately, the dream might imply that you need a vacation or a break.

ocean: A dream of the ocean often represents the emotional setting of your life. The context of the dream is important here. Sailing through rough seas suggests you are capable of dealing with life's ups and downs. Large waves can also represent untapped powers of the unconscious. Fishing in the ocean and catching something big can suggest an opportunity is at hand or that you are delving into the wealth of your unconscious. To be lost at sea might indicate you have lost your moorings, that you are adrift in life and in need of direction. To be anchored in the ocean might indicate you have found a place in life.

October: To dream of October portends success. New friendships or business affairs will ripen into lasting relationships.

officer: An officer, whether military, police, or corporate, represents an authority figure. Dreaming of an officer, especially if you don't know the person, can suggest a fear or wariness of authority figures or a need for guidance from a person with authority.

oil: A dream of oil represents great wealth or inner wealth, as in a dream of pumping crude oil to the surface. Using aromatic oils in a dream can represent sacred matters. A person associated with oil might be slick, or a smooth-talker.

old man: If the old man guides or directs you in some way, he is, in Jungian thought, an archetypal figure. If the man appears to be weak or injured in some way, he could symbolize some part of yourself that needs attention or someone in your life who needs your help. It could also mean that you need to redefine your beliefs about aging.

old woman: In Jungian terms, an old woman is an archetypal symbol of the power of the feminine, or the gatekeeper between life and death. If she is weak or injured, she may represent a part of yourself that needs attention or someone in your life who needs your help.

onyx: According to traditional dream keys, onyx portends arguments.

otter: Dreaming of an otter warns of frisky behavior that causes you to overlook something important.

oven: An oven might represent a gestation period. It also symbolizes the womb and feminine energy. A dream of an oven could relate to a pregnancy.

owl: An owl represents both wisdom and mystery and is a symbol of the unconscious. And, since owls have excellent night vision, they might also signify illumination for a dark situation. In addition, owls symbolize messages and news; pay attention to your inner voice in reacting to these missives. If, in your dream, you hear an owl screech, it means you will be shocked with bad news. (See also *cat*.)

ox: To dream of an ox implies great strength and endurance and an ability to carry on against great odds.

painting: If a wall is being painted, the act might suggest that something is being hidden or covered up. Painting at an easel could indicate artistic or creative talents are ready to be expressed.

palm tree: A dream about palm trees denotes that you are in a hopeful situation and happiness will soon be yours. If a woman dreams of an avenue of palms, she will have a cheerful home and faithful husband.

paradise: Whatever your idea of paradise is—the Garden of Eden; a double-header on a Saturday afternoon; beer and hot dogs; watching VH1 all day—just imagine a perfect world and you are in paradise. If you dream you are in paradise, it means all your friends are loyal. If you are a mother and dream you are in paradise, your children will be fair and obedient.

park: Dreaming of a park might suggest a wish to relax and enjoy life. Walking in an unlit park at night might mean that you are delving into areas of darkness and danger, or that you are dealing with hidden or mysterious matters.

parsley: Dreaming of parsley means you will attain success and be surrounded by healthy and lively people. To dream of eating parsley is a sign of good health.

party: To find yourself at a party in a dream suggests that a celebration is in order. If you are concerned about a particular matter that remains unsettled, the dream might indicate a favorable resolution.

past lovers: Many sexual dreams are a commentary on your past and present relationships, and dreams that feature past lovers are no exception. In outrageous dream circumstances, all of your past lovers might even show up at the same party, or in the same bed. This sort of dream is an indication that you need to analyze past involvements that continue to impact current relationships. If you have a dream of this sort, it's important to look for patterns that mark your relationships. This is especially critical if you've had a series of unsuccessful relationships or affairs that began filled with promise and ended badly.

pasture: If you dream of a pasture freshly plowed and ready for planting, a long struggle will soon be resolved and you will have great success.

path: In dreams, the appearance of a path indicates the course of your spiritual progress. Make note of the path's condition in your dream. Is it well tended? Filled with rocks or holes? This condition should be highly indicative of how smoothly your path is progressing.

peacock: A dream that includes a peacock suggests being egotistical and that you have something to show off or a reason to be proud, similar to the peacock that displays its colorful tail feathers.

pearls: If you dream of owning pearls, you will have success in business and be highly regarded in society. If a woman dreams she receives pearls from a lover, she should be prepared for festive occasions. This also denotes she will select a faithful and loving husband. If you dream of a string of pearls breaking, watch out for suffering, sadness, and sorrow.

pears: If you are admiring pears on a tree, the future looks promising—more promising than it did previously. Dreaming of pears does not always mean a future of success, however: Eating pears in a dream portends poor success and ill health.

pepper: If you dream of pepper burning your tongue, you will suffer as a result of your friends gossiping about you.

photocopy machine: As odd as a dream about this object might seem, don't overlook its meaning. Yes, if you're having a tough time at work and you dream of battling the office copy machine this could represent your career struggles. But a dream of a photocopy machine might have a deeper meaning. Keep in mind that photocopiers spit out identical copies of whatever you put in. Think about whether this dream might represent a fear you have about becoming just like everyone else or losing your individuality.

photograph: Since a photograph is an image of a person or object rather than the real thing, a dream of a photograph hints of deception. If you recognize a person in a dream photo, be careful in your dealings with the person and look for hidden meaning in the person's actions. To dream of having your own photograph made suggests that you might unwittingly be the cause of your own troubles.

physician: A physician appearing in a dream might indicate that a healing is at hand. A physician is also an authority figure who might be offering a diagnosis on some matter. Sometimes, a physician might take the form of a trusted friend who isn't a doctor but whose nurturing traits are healing. (See also *doctor* and *nurse*.)

piano: Music in general represents joyous or festive feelings. Note the condition and type of music coming from the piano. A broken piano symbolizes displeasure in your achievements; an old-fashioned piano suggests neglect over a matter at hand.

pig: Dreaming of a pig symbolizes overcoming something and beginning anew.

pill: Taking a pill in a dream suggests that the dreamer might be required to go along with something unpleasant, but positive results should follow.

pilot: A pilot symbolizes someone soaring high and in control in spite of the fast pace. A dream of a pilot may represent that you're in the pilot's seat concerning some issue in your life.

pink: If your dream includes the color pink, this is an indication of good health. This significance is not surprising—just consider that widely accepted notion of the "healthy glow" of rosy pink cheeks.

pit: The idea of a dark, bottomless pit is related to other dream symbols that represent unknown emptiness. Dreaming of a pit is typically an indication that you are faced with obstacles, fear of failure, or some sort of other uncertainty. (See also *abyss*, *chasm*, *cliff*, and *precipice*.)

planet: Seeing a planet or visiting another planet in a dream might indicate a new adventure, a new way of thinking, or a new dimension of creativity.

pleasure: A dream about pleasure—a feeling of gratification—means you will have many financial and personal gains of enjoyment.

plums: Dreaming of ripe plums indicates that you will have a joyous occasion to attend. If you dream of eating plums, expect a flirtatious affair. If you are gathering plums in your dream, it signifies that you will obtain all your desires.

polar bear: These creatures can represent some sort of trickery or deceit that is upon you. Maybe one of your enemies will appear as a friend to overcome you. However, seeing the skin of a polar bear suggests that you will successfully triumph over adversity.

police: Police officers represent authority; they uphold the law. A dream of the police might serve as a warning against breaking the law or bending rules. It might suggest a fear of punishment. Alternately, the dream could indicate a desire for justice and a need to punish the wrongdoers in a matter of concern.

pond: A pond signifies tranquility and a placid outlook in either the dreamer or a person in the dream.

porcupine: A dream that includes a porcupine warns that you should be on guard.

precipice: Standing on the edge of a precipice represents a fear of falling into emptiness or the unknown. This is a dream of obstacles and uncertainty. (See also *abyss*, *chasm*, *cliff*, and *pit*.)

pregnant: If a woman dreams of being pregnant, it could indicate a desire for a child or the onset of the condition. A pregnancy could also symbolize something new coming into being in the dreamer's life, an idea or project that is gestating.

president of the United States: Not as uncommon as it might seem, to talk with the president of the United States in a dream can represent an interest in lofty ideals or political matters, or a strong desire to be a politician.

priest: A priest can be a symbol of a benign spiritual authority who serves as a guide. A representative of your inner voice that acts as a spiritual escort, the appearance of a priest in your dreams is perhaps a call to consider embarking on spiritual studies. Alternately, a priest might symbolize a dictatorial figure or one who judges and condemns. A dream of a priest can indicate the need to follow or eschew conventional religion. Look to surrounding details for clarification.

primrose: In dreams, primroses herald new friendships.

prison: Constraint and restriction are implied. If you see yourself at work in a prison, the dream might suggest that you've limited your creativity or that you feel it's difficult to "escape" your job for a better one.

profanity: If you dream of profanity, or blasphemy, for that matter—more specifically, taking God's name in vain—it denotes that you are cultivating coarse traits. If you dream others are blasting you with profanity, this indicates that you are in for some rough times.

professor: A professor can represent knowledge, wisdom, and higher education.

prophet: A prophet provides knowledge, guidance, and perhaps a peek at the future. Or, the symbol could indicate that you're in need of guidance.

puddle: Stepping into or stomping through puddles represents a parting or clearing away of troubles, with good times to follow. To dream that you are just wetting your feet in a puddle might mean that trouble will follow a pleasurable experience.

pump: To see a pump in a dream denotes that energy is available to meet your needs. A functioning pump could also symbolize good health. A broken pump signifies a breakdown or disruption of the usual way of doing things.

pumpkin: A signature fruit of the autumn harvest, pumpkins are often associated with bounty, fulfillment, and Thanksgiving. Carved into jack-o-lanterns and illuminated on Halloween, they also have a magical element to them.

puppet: A dream of a puppet might indicate that you are feeling manipulated in some aspect of your life. Alternately, if you are behind the puppet, the dream could be warning you that you're acting in a manipulative manner.

purse: Purses usually contain credit cards, money, and identification—society's evidence of who you are. Therefore, it's no surprise that a dream involving this item represents concern about your identity and, perhaps more specifically, a shift in your identity. For example, author Gayle Delaney notes, this dream sometimes occurs among women whose kids have recently left home. This analysis can just as easily apply for you if you are in the midst of any other sort of transition from one way of life or mode of thought to another. (See also *wallet*.)

quarrel: A dream of a quarrel might indicate that an inner turmoil is plaguing you. If the person you're quarreling with is identifiable, consider the relationship you have with the person and see if you can identify the area of disagreement. There could be clues in the dream that indicate a way to resolve the differences.

queen: Both an authority and a mother figure, the queen is an archetypal symbol of power. If you are the queen, the dream could be suggesting a desire for leadership. If someone else is the queen, the dream might indicate that you see the woman as capable and powerful.

quest: A dream of a quest can indicate a desire to achieve a goal or embark on an adventure.

quicksand: A dream of quicksand indicates that you need to watch where you are headed. If you're already in the quicksand, then you're probably mired in an emotional matter and feel as if you can't escape. It could refer to either business or personal matters.

quilt: A quilt suggests warmth and protection. A patchwork quilt symbolizes the sewing together of various aspects of your life to form a protective covering.

R

rabbit: The rabbit is a symbol of abundance, creativity, overall luck, fertility, and magic, as the rabbit pulled from the magician's hat. Although fertility could relate literally to the conception of children, it might also have other figurative connotations, such as financial abundance, the success of a particular project, or other matters. A white rabbit might signify faithfulness in love.

Black Rabbits

Rabbits played a key symbolic role for Edith, a French-Canadian massage therapist, who was feeling depressed when she had the following dream:

I'm in a school gymnasium, but there are no bleachers. It's a large, open room with lots of cages. I go over to the cages and see that they are filled with black rabbits. There are hundreds of them, but they are all dead.

I'm horrified at what I see. Then I notice an older man nearby. When I tell him that the rabbits are dead, he doesn't seem concerned. He says he can redo them for me. It won't be a problem. When I look again, I'm surprised to see that the cages are filled with black rabbits, more than before, and they're moving about and very much alive.

At the time of this dream, Edith had recently ended a bad relationship and was feeling depressed when she called her father one

continued on following page

race: If you are racing in a dream, then perhaps you're involved in an overly competitive situation or you're in a rush. The message might be that it's time to slow down and relax.

rain: A fresh downpour symbolizes a washing or cleansing away of the old. Alternately, a rainy day might indicate a gloomy situation. To hear the patter of rain on the roof can signify domestic bliss, while seeing a downpour of rain

continued from previous page

night. She told him that she felt dead inside, that no matter how hard she tried to keep a positive attitude, it wasn't working.

Her father, also a massage therapist, is known in Quebec for his healing touch. He asked her if her third vertebra was sore and she said that it was. He told her that he would work on it in the astral plane while she slept, and that she would feel much better.

The next morning Edith didn't notice much change and although she felt somewhat better during the day, she went to bed again feeling empty and dead inside. Then she had the black rabbit dream. The following morning she felt much better.

She interpreted the black rabbits as a symbol of magic and good luck. The fact that they were alive, for Edith, meant that the magic in her unconscious mind had been revived. She felt elated and called her father. He said he'd worked on her spine in the astral plane on the same night she'd had the rabbit dream.

from inside a house could represent requited love and fortune. Seeing it rain on others might mean that you are excluding friends from your confidence.

rainbow: Usually seen after rainstorms in nature, their appearance in dreams might signify that favorable conditions will arise after a brief period of unpleasantness. Seeing a low-hanging rainbow over verdant trees can intimate success in any endeavor.

rams: If you dream of a ram charging you with its head down, it indicates that you are under attack from some quarter. If the ram is near, it might mean that the attack is near or that you will have little time to react. A ram charging from a distance suggests that you will have time to respond to the situation. Consider whether someone in your life is trying to "ram" something down your throat. If the ram is quietly grazing in a pasture, the indication could be that you have powerful allies on your side.

rapids: Rapids represent danger and a fear of being swept away by emotions.

rat: Rats are generally associated with filth and dilapidation. Dreaming of a rat or rats might suggest the deterioration of a situation. Ask yourself who the "rat" is in your life. Since rats can also be a symbol for difficult changes, go with this theme and consider if there are any changes in your life taking place that you fear are deteriorating. (See also *death*.)

raven: In dreams, ravens represent some sort of warning.

red: The color red is often associated with vitality and energy, the heart, and blood. In a dream, the color red can also mean anger or strong emotions, as in "seeing red." Red often indicates that the dream originates from the deepest level of your being.

referee: A referee in a dream can symbolize an inner battle taking place or it can relate to conflict in your daily life. Can you identify the issue? If so, weigh the two sides, negotiate, and reach a settlement. Sometimes working with a third party who is not involved in the dispute can help.

religion: If you should dream about religion—particularly the religion in which you were raised—and in your dream you are discussing that religion, it indicates your business affairs will be disagreeable. Also watch out for much adversity.

religious devotion: If you dream of religious devotion, watch out for deceit in business. If, however, you are a farmer and dream of being religious and devout, it signifies you will have a good harvest. If a woman dreams of being religiously devout, it denotes she is chaste and she will have an adoring husband.

religious revival: Dreaming that you are attending a religious revival signifies a family disturbance is about to happen and you will have unprofitable engagements. If you dream you take part in the revival, you will receive much displeasure from your friends.

ribbons: If you should dream of ribbons floating from the costume of another person, you will have happy and pleasant friendships and everyday cares will not be troubling. To dream of buying ribbons denotes a happy life. Dreaming of decorating yourself with ribbons signifies you will soon have a good offer of marriage.

rice: Rice is the dietary staple of the majority of the world's population. To dream of rice is a symbol of fertility and good fortune.

river: A dream of floating down a river might indicate a lack of motivation. Are you allowing surrounding circumstances to direct your life, rather than taking charge? A dream of a surging, frothing river can also relate to deep-seated anger. In mythology, a river sometimes relates to death or the passing from one state to another.

road: A road is a means of getting from one place to another. Notice the condition of the road in your dream: A smooth and straight road suggests the path ahead is easy. On the other hand, a road with dips and curves could indicate that you need to be aware, flexible, and ready for change. A roadblock suggests that there are detours in your path.

robin: One of the first birds to be spotted at the end of the winter, the robin is typically a sign of spring.

rooster: To dream of a rooster indicates that you will be successful and rise to places of great honor.

rose: A rose symbolizes the feminine and is associated with romance, beauty, and love. A dream of someone handing you a rose might indicate an offering of love. A rose can also relate to good and evil. If someone crushes a rose, that person's intent might be wicked.

rosemary: A dream involving the herb rosemary portends sadness and indifference will cause unhappiness in your home, even though everything appears prosperous.

rubies: A dream about a ruby means that your speculation in love or business will turn out well. If you dream of losing a ruby however, your lover will soon be indifferent to you.

ruins: To dream of something in ruins suggests the deterioration of some condition in your life. Keep in mind that when things fall apart an opportunity to rebuild inevitably appears. If you are planning a trip, especially one to another culture, a dream of ancient ruins could symbolize the adventure of the journey ahead. Alternately, it could signify that you have the ability to access knowledge or wisdom from the past.

running: When you run in a dream, it can be either toward or away from something; you might want to escape from something or to reach toward a goal. Depending on the circumstances, the dream might indicate that you need to hurry, or that you're rushing around too much and need to rest. Are you running alone or with others? The former might symbolize that you will overcome your competition in business matters, while the latter might represent your participation in a joyous occasion.

If you dream of running, not from a predator, but running for exercise, that means that you are moving toward a pleasant and successful life.

S

sacrifice: To see yourself sacrificed in a dream suggests that you're giving up something important for the sake of others. Closely examine your feelings about the matter. Decide what changes, if any, need to be made in your life and in your relationships.

sage: To dream of sage indicates thrift and economy will be practiced in your family. Women dreaming of sage will know a useless extravagance in love and fortune.

sailor: A dream of a sailor suggests that you are working on a ship. Symbolically, it could mean that you are working on matters dealing with the unconscious or emotions. (See also *ship* and *water*.)

saint: A saint in a dream indicates you're being guided or are seeking guidance from a higher source.

salt: This staple can represent the need to purify, banish, or preserve something. Dreaming of salt generally signifies unhappy surroundings.

To dream of eating salt portends that everything will go awry and quarrels will arise in your family circle. If a young woman dreams of eating salt, this indicates that her lover will desert her for a more beautiful woman.

sapphires: Dreaming of a sapphire denotes continuous good fortune.

scent: If you smell something pleasant in your dream, then generally it represents something pleasant or positive. If, on the other hand, you have a dream that includes a terrible stench, this is an indication that you are in the midst of some sort of distasteful or unpleasant change/transition in your life. (See also *death*.)

school: A dream of school might indicate that you are gaining knowledge at a deep level of your existence or that what you are learning in your waking life is being processed and adapted by the unconscious. What happens in the school is important in the interpretation. If you're late to class or show up to take a test without ever having gone to class, the dream is a common symbol for feeling unprepared for something in your life. If you're looking for a school or classroom, the dream could be telling you that expanding your education is in order.

scissors: This could mean there is something in your life you want to cut off. Dreaming of scissors also might indicate a need to "cut it out." Pay attention to the person holding the scissors in your dream—in that case, the scissors could be a symbol for someone in your life who is acting "snippy."

scrapbook: Scrapbooks are full of things from the past that are tucked away and forgotten. Note the other details of your dream: Are you viewing a scrapbook with someone? What are you placing in the scrapbook? Seeing a scrapbook in your dream might suggest that you have an unpleasant situation that needs to be put in the past.

screaming without sound: If you dream of yelling, and yet no sound comes out, it's probably associated with an instance in your waking life where you feel unable to voice your feelings. Think about whether you have any concerns weighing on your mind or feelings about specific people or situations in your life that you feel uneasy speaking up about, and consider how you can begin taking steps to help you "find" your voice and express yourself.

sea: Dreams of the sea represent unfulfilled longings or unchanging emotions.

September: Dreaming of September represents good luck and fortune.

searching: Dreams that involve searching are usually less about the thing you are searching for, although that could provide you with contextual clues, and more about the search itself. Searching in a dream is typically a metaphor for something you are looking for—or something you need—in your waking life. If, for instance, you have a dream in which you are searching for a place to make love, where you search from house to house, place to place, or town to town, the dream is more about the search for a place than about sex itself. Such dreams are a metaphor for a search for intimacy.

sex: According to Sigmund Freud, all of our dreams are linked with sexual issues. Freud was writing during the Victorian era, when talk of sex was taboo, and his ideas helped free the Western world from the repressive strictures of the era. However, Freud's view that the sex drive powers virtually all of our dreams is no longer accepted. In fact, it's now thought by a number of dream researchers that some sex dreams might not have anything at all to do with sex.

Sexual dreams can contain clues to important personal needs, desires, fears, and changes. For instance, people recovering from illness, depression, surgery, or the grieving process, might suddenly and inexplicably begin having sexual dreams. Such dreams appear to be associated with an increase in physical vitality and a greater sense of aliveness, although they might precede physical recovery in some cases. Dreams such as this often come across as almost humorous, given recent physical challenges. Yet, these dreams serve as reminders that although you've been through hell, you're still very much alive.

sex dreams where parents appear: If you've had a sex dream in which one or both of your parents have appeared, ask yourself if there is some belief, fear, or expectation you learned from your parent(s) that tends to intrude into your awareness as you begin to make love. Is

there a sense in which you believe your fulfillment might be disloyal or damaging to your parents? If in this sort of dream you are more worried
about your parents' presence than about your
sexual fulfillment, this might be an indication that
you worry about their opinions more than is ob-
jectively necessary.

sex in a public place: If you dream of making
love in a public place, and especially if your per-
formance is observed by others, this dream dramatically calls attention to a public action in your
life. Consider things you've recently done in public—or those things you are about to do. Examine
the event carefully. Also look at other aspects of
the dream itself. Who is your partner? How is that
person involved in the public event in your waking life? If the person has no connection with the
event, then what does that person symbolize?
These sorts of contextual clues will help you to
decipher the broader meaning of the dream.

sex with a celebrity: Such sex dreams,
sometimes suggested to your mind in your waking life—after seeing a certain actor in a TV show
or movie, for example—can fulfill a fantasy or enhance your love life. Dreams in which you are

The Vanishing Lover

Dreams that involve sex often have tremendous symbolic value beyond the physical action. In the following example, the dreamer, Bill, was a thirty-three-year-old engineer who had never been married. The situation speaks volumes about his tendency in romantic relationships.

Everything starts out great. I'm with Sharon, a woman I've known through business for several months. I'm very attracted to her and now we're in a romantic setting. We both know what we want and neither of us has any inhibitions. But just as I become fully aroused, Sharon starts to disappear. All of my efforts to keep her from vanishing fail. Sharon simply evaporates.

For Bill, the meaning of the dream is more about a pattern in his life than a statement about Sharon. He has rarely had a sexual relationship last longer than a few months. Part of Bill's problem, he admits, is that he only likes the exciting early sexual encounters with a new mate. Once the woman starts to become part of his life, his interest fades.

making love to a famous person can also be related to your desire to achieve success in the world in which the famous person has starred. A budding writer might dream of sleeping with a bestselling author, a struggling athlete might dream of marrying a well-known professional athlete, and a beginning television reporter might dream of sleeping with a famous broadcaster.

sexual frustration: If you dream you are making love, but in your dream you stop short of climax, you're left unfulfilled. If you have a sexual dream that starts out promising, but then just fizzles out, leaving you frustrated and angry, this dream symbolizes a lack of fulfillment and a frustration in life that may have nothing at all to do with your sex life. Look at recent events in your life, and consider those things that have left you frustrated.

sexual inhibition: "If you find yourself enjoying sex in a dream in circumstances your waking mind finds shocking, this is a sure sign that you are imposing a lifestyle on yourself which is at variance with your natural feelings in some way, and your dream is a warning to change it," says Ann Faraday in *The Dream Game*. "The most important thing . . . is to become aware of one's own feelings, thereby avoiding the danger of the repressed impulses seeking expression in some devious way, perhaps by outbursts of anger against one's partner or by 'accidentally' finding oneself in some compromising situation with the dream lover in waking life."

A common dream that deals with sexual inhibitions is one in which one or both of your parents walk in on you while you are making love. In such a dream, your parent might talk to you as if there is nothing unusual about his or her appearance in your bedroom. An important aspect of the dream is the identity of your partner. If it's your spouse, consider whether your parents approve of your spouse, or whether you feel a need for such approval.

shadow: This is another one of Jung's archetypes. Dreaming of your shadow might suggest that you need to address hidden parts of yourself. Perhaps you do not accept these darker aspects of your personality and project them onto others. The dream might also suggest that you need to incorporate the shadow side into your psyche.

Shakespeare: To dream of William Shakespeare doesn't portend good luck—unhappiness and despondency will loom, causing you anxiety and your love will be stripped of passion. If you dream of reading Shakespeare, however, you will attach yourself to literary accomplishments.

shaking hands: The handshake marks either a new beginning or an ending to a situation. Are you saying farewell to someone in a dream? Then perhaps you are saying goodbye to a matter at hand. To dream of shaking hands with a prominent leader might mean you will be held in esteem by strangers in a new situation.

shaving: Is there something in your life that needs to be cleaned up or removed? To dream of shaving yourself connotes that you are in charge of your future. Shaving with a dull razor suggests a troublesome or painful issue. A clean-shaven countenance suggests a smooth journey through a matter at hand.

sheep: If you dream of a sheep, consider whether or not you perceive yourself to be one of a flock. This can be a comforting image if it sparks a sense of community. However, it might also indicate that you lack individuality or the will to strike out on your own. In that case, sheep symbolize passiveness that can lead to undoing.

shell: A shell usually symbolizes a womb. Depending on the circumstances of the dream, it can portend a birth of a child or a new project. A shell can also symbolize protection, as in something you retreat into, like a turtle or snail, when you feel threatened.

ship: Since a ship travels on water, the dream could signify a voyage through the unconscious or a journey involving your emotions. The state of the ship and the condition of the water should be considered in the interpretation. To see a ship in a storm might indicate your concern over a tempestuous or unfortunate affair, either in business or personal matters. To dream of others shipwrecked could symbolize a feeling of inadequacy in protecting friends or family. (See also *sailor.*)

shoes: Shoes are a means of moving ahead. Shiny, new shoes might suggest a journey is about to begin. Well-worn shoes, on the other hand, might indicate that one is weary of the journey or that it is near completion. Mismatched shoes might indicate that the journey is multifaceted. Also consider the old cliché: "If the shoe fits, wear it."

shovel: A tool for digging, a shovel in a dream might indicate that you are searching for something or are about to embark on a quest for inner knowledge. A shovel might also represent labor or hard work ahead. A broken shovel could mean that you are experiencing frustration in your work.

shower: To dream of taking a shower can symbolize a spiritual renewal. It might also signify a bonus or reward showered upon the dreamer.

sickness/illness: If you dream of being ill, ask yourself if you're in need of being cared for and pampered. This dream might also be a message to watch your health. To dream of a family member who is sick represents some misfortune or issue that is troubling your domestic life.

silk: If you dream of wearing silk clothing, your high ambitions will be met. If you dream of old silk, it means you are feeling pride in your ancestors and also that you will soon be courted by a wealthy, but elderly person.

singing: Hearing singing in a dream signifies a pleasant and cheerful attitude. It also suggests that you might hear promising news regarding a matter at hand. If you are singing in the dream, note the type (happy, sad) of song you are singing.

sister: Like a dream of a *brother*, sisters also conjure images of family closeness and security juxtaposed with the familiar notion of sibling rivalry. In dreams, sisters often represent the sensitive, caring, and nurturing side of the personality, especially if the image is of a protective older sister. Like a brother image in a dream, a younger sister might also represent a more vulnerable side.

skating: Dreaming of skating could signify to the dreamer that they are gliding over a matter at hand, or that they might be skating on thin ice. Note all aspects of the dream to get a better sense of what it is indicating.

skull: To dream of a skull and crossbones is a traditional sign of danger and possibly death—a warning.

sky: Dreaming of the sky symbolizes hope, vitality, and a creative force.

smoke: If you dream of smoke filling a room, it suggests that a matter in your life is being obscured. On the other hand, if the smoke is dissipating, clarity is imminent.

snake: A snake is an archetypal image that can suggest numerous interpretations. In mythology, snakes are symbols of wisdom and fertility. In the ancient Greek and Roman cultures, snakes were also symbols of the healing arts. Like lizards, snakes shed their skin—a symbol of renewal. Therefore, dreaming of a snake could also mean that some type of new life or opportunity is going to begin. In fact, according to some Eastern traditions, the snake is related to a power that rises from the base of the spine and is a symbol of transformation. For example, the ancient symbol of the snake swallowing its own tail represents the way nature feeds on and renews itself.

However, snakes also often symbolize the dangers of the underworld. In the Bible, the snake symbolizes temptation, forbidden knowledge, and the source of evil. Snakes often appear in fairy tales as tricksters who are wise but wily. The Freudian interpretation relates snakes to the male genitalia, and in dreams snakes are also linked to wisdom or sex, or both. When trying to interpret a dream about a snake, pay attention to how you view snakes symbolically and consider other aspects of the dream.

Jung considered the archetypal image of snakes to represent an awareness of the essential energy of life and nature.

Snake in the Grass

As previously mentioned in this book, archetypes are symbols or themes commonly recognized by the "collective consciousness," and held in common by many cultures. In the following dream, snakes, a typical archetypal symbol, hold a strong meaning for the dreamer.

I'm walking in tall grass, grass that brushes my knees. I hear rustling around me and pick up my pace, anxious to get to the clearing I can see just ahead. I know the rustling is caused by snakes.

The rustling gets louder, like the cacophony of a thousand crickets screaming for rain. I start running. I'm still running when I reach the clearing and run right into a bed of snakes. They are everywhere, writhing, slithering, rattling. But even worse than the snakes is the realization that I'm barefoot and that the only way I'm going to get out of this is to walk through them.

So I walk. And I make it through the bed of snakes without getting bitten.

continued on following page

snow: Snow can represent purity if seen in a pristine landscape. Since snow is a solidified form of water, it can also stand for frozen emotions. If the snow is melting, the suggestion is that frozen feelings are thawing. To find yourself in a snowstorm might represent uncertainty in an emotional matter, or sorrow in failing to enjoy some long expected pleasure. Dreaming of snowcapped mountains in the distance suggests that *continued from previous page*

The woman who had this dream was breaking away from her Catholic background to explore areas that the religion of her childhood would call heretical. Therefore, she interpreted this dream to mean that although this exploration was somewhat frightening for her, she would complete it without "harm." She felt the dream was confirming her belief that the exploration was a necessary step in her growth as a human being.

On another level, though, she felt the dream was pointing to a situation at work, one in which she was surrounded by "snakes in the grass"—a pun that probably indicated malicious gossip. Because the snakes didn't bite her, she surmised she would survive whatever was being said about her. So, in this case, not only is the snake an archetypal symbol, it also had strong relevance to her personally, and resonated in her daily life.

your ambitions will yield no advancement. Eating snow symbolizes a failure to realize ideals.

son: To dream of a son when you don't have one might simply be an indication of your desire for children. If you do have a son, your dreams might represent elements of yourself as a child or your own sense of responsibility as a parent. (See also *daughter*.)

space: Seeing a vast expanse of outer space in your dreams, as opposed to a single star or small star grouping, can be an alternative abyss dream. In the tarot, the abyss is part of the fool's journey to enlightenment. Therefore, a dream of space might indicate that you are on the verge of a leap into the unknown—you are at the point where you simply need to dive in to something and trust your instincts and capabilities. (See also *abyss*.)

spaceship: A spaceship in a dream might suggest a journey into the unknown. It could also symbolize a spiritual quest.

spear: Thrusting a spear at someone in a dream could represent an effort to thrust your will on another person. If the spear is hurled over a field, toward a mountain or an ocean, the dream might mean that you are making a powerful statement to the world.

spider: In dreams, spiders, industrious and detailed in their web-spinning, can symbolize a careful and energetic approach to your work. They also suggest that you will be pleasantly rewarded for your labors. To dream of a spider spinning its web signifies that your homelife will be happy and secure. If there are many spiders in your dream, it represents good health and friends. A confrontation with a large spider could signify a quick ascent to fame and fortune, unless the large spider bites you, in which it may represent the loss of money or reputation.

spring: The season that arrives each year on the heels of winter is often associated with birth, freshness, full blooms, and new life. If you dream of spring, ask yourself if anything new is "blooming" in your life, or where you might be encountering new births. Remember, birth is not always synonymous with the birth of a child. Any sort of creative endeavor, work or home project, or even a new task or hobby that you undertake can relate to the symbols of birth and new life.

squirrel: To see these friendly creatures in a dream might mean that pleasant acquaintances will soon visit, or that you will advance in business.

stage: If you dream of being on stage and forgetting your lines in front of a full theater of people, this is an example of a classic fear or anxiety dream. Like a dream of failing a test in school, this sort of dream generally reflects a feeling of being unprepared. It can also relate to a feeling of being exposed in public and judged by those around you.

stairs: Climbing a stairway in a dream can mean that you are on your way to achieving a goal. Descending a flight of stairs, or falling down one, might indicate a fall in prestige or economic status. To sit on a step could suggest that you are pausing in your everyday life with its challenges to consider where things stand.

stars: When a star or stars appear in your dreams, this can mean a variety of things. Stars might denote realized or unrealized wishes, dreams, and hopes, or a tendency toward overly romantic outlooks—as in the old cliché of being "starry-eyed." Dreaming of a star could also represent goals that might or might not be obtainable—reaching for the stars, in other words. Remember that the traditional fairy godmother usually waves a wand with a star at its tip, so don't rule out these sorts of fanciful associations, either. If the star in your dreams has five points, it could be an alternative pentacle, which denotes spiritual or magickal matters that you should watch.

On a different note, stars can be a symbol of good health. Finally, stars might also represent outside influences impressing themselves on a situation (akin to astrological influences).

statue: Dreaming of a statue or statues could signify a lack of movement in your life. Statues are also cold and can symbolize frozen feelings.

stillborn: To dream of a stillborn infant indicates a premature ending or some distressing circumstance in a matter at hand.

stones: Stones can represent small irritations or obstacles that must be overcome. Seeing yourself throw a stone in a dream could mean that you have cause to reprove someone. If the stone stands alone in your dream, often it represents the self.

storm: To dream of an approaching storm indicates emotional turmoil in some aspect of your life. Dark skies and thunder might also be a forewarning that danger is approaching. Alternately, a storm could symbolize rapid changes occurring in your life.

suicide: A dream of killing yourself probably is a symbolic reflection of what's going on in your conscious life. Such a dream might reflect a personal transformation, a divorce, changing careers, or other major life shifts. You are essentially killing your past, becoming a new person.

summer: The season of warmth and ripening to fruition, summer is one of the most enjoyable times of the year. If you dream of summer, it probably hints of good times and fun. Also, since summer is a growing season, it can also represent a time of laying the proper foundations and then cultivating those things that need tending, with the hope of completion and actualization that follows in autumn.

sun: Dreaming of the sun is usually fortuitous. The sun is a symbol of light, warmth, good health, and energy. The sun rises in the morning and is associated with awakening. It is a symbol for what author Layne Dalfen calls the "action" phase, when you have reflected on what you need to and are now ready to put that knowledge to work for you.

In Native American lore, the sun symbolizes the father or the masculine principal.

swimming: A dream of swimming suggests the dreamer is immersed in an exploration of emotional matters or the unconscious.

sword: A sword is a symbol of strength and power. It also can cut to the bone. Dreaming of a sword might suggest that aggressive action is required. An alternative to an athame, the sword wields greater power and therefore bears greater responsibility. (See also *athame*.)

synagogue: If you dream of seeing a synagogue off in the distance, it means your enemies are preventing you from acquiring a fortune. If you climb to the top of the outside of the synagogue, you soon will overcome any opposition to you.

table: To dream of an empty table might suggest a concern about a lack or shortage of possessions, while a table covered with food might symbolize a time of abundance.

tambourine: The appearance of a tambourine symbolizes pleasure in some unusual undertaking about to take place.

tassels: To dream of tassels means you will reach the peak of your desires. However, dreaming of losing tassels means you might go through unpleasant experiences.

tattoo: Tattoos are associated with the strange and exotic. To dream of seeing your body tattooed suggests that some difficulty will cause you to have a long absence from home or familiar surroundings. Dreaming that you are a tattooist suggests that your desire for some strange experience might alienate you from friends.

teeth: A dream about losing teeth might be a literal warning about your dental condition. But if you've had a checkup, then you should consider that the dream might be telling you something about yourself.

Teeth are what you use to bite. If you lose your bite, you lose power. Losing teeth might also symbolize a loss of face or spoiled self-image. It could also be a metaphor for "loose" or careless speech. Note the other aspects of the dream. For example, to examine your teeth suggests that you exercise caution in a matter at hand. To clean your teeth represents that some struggle is necessary to keep your standing. Admiring your teeth for their whiteness suggests that wishes for a pleasant occupation and happiness will be fulfilled. To dream that you pull your own teeth and are feeling around the cavity with your tongue signifies your trepidation over a situation into which you are about to enter. Dreaming of imperfect teeth is one of the worst dreams to have for it connotes bad feelings about your appearance and well-being.

If those meanings don't work for you, however, ask yourself what teeth mean to you. Do they represent power? A nice appearance? Aggressiveness? What is it, exactly, that makes you feel "toothless"?

telephone: A telephone might symbolize the attempt to contact the unconscious. If the phone is ringing and no one is answering, the dream might suggest that you are ignoring the call of your unconscious.

tent: A tent provides shelter and is usually associated with camping. A dream of a tent could indicate that you are in need of a getaway, a retreat from everyday life.

thaw: Thawing represents the rebirth or return to pleasant conditions. To dream of seeing ice thaw might symbolize that something or someone giving you trouble will soon yield pleasure and profit.

thief: If you dream of someone stealing something, the implication is that something is being taken from you. It does not necessarily have to be a theft of actual goods. It could also be something more abstract, such as a boss or colleague who is stealing your energy or ideas. If you're the thief, the message could be a warning that you are taking what you don't deserve and that you should change your ways.

thirst: A dream in which you are thirsty suggests that you are in need of nourishment, either physical, mental, or emotional. To see others re-lieving their thirst suggests that this nourishment might come from others.

thorn: A thorn can represent an annoyance of some sort—in other words, "a thorn in your side."

tiger: Tigers symbolize courage, compe-tence, and tenacity. Aggressive and fierce in the wild, seeing these animals in a dream might sym-bolize that you are under persecution or will be tormented. However, if you see yourself fending off an attack, this could mean that you will be ex-tremely successful in all your ventures.

tornado: Swift and terrible agents of destruc-tion in nature, a dream involving a tornado sug-gests that your desire for a quick resolution in a matter at hand could lead to disappointment.

torrent: To dream of a seething torrent of wa-ter suggests a profound unrest in the emotional state of the dreamer or a person in the dream.

tower: To dream of a tower could symbolize vigilance, as a watchtower, or punishment or iso-lation as a guard tower. Dreaming of being in an "ivory tower" indicates that you or the subject of your dream is out of touch with the everyday world.

train: A train symbolizes a journey. Look at the other elements in the dream to understand the nature of your journey. If the train isn't moving, the dream might be suggesting some impediment in your life. If you can't find your luggage, the dream might indicate that you are concerned that you're not ready for this journey. If you are on a smoothly running train, but there are no tracks, the dream might signify that you are concerned over some affair that will eventually be

Missing Connections

The following dream about being on a train, recounted by a newspaper reporter named Jerry, relates to travel and missed connections:

I'm taking a train in a foreign country and must transfer from one train to another. The problem is that I've lost track of my luggage. I'm looking all over for it, and I know I must hurry or I'll miss the connecting train. Sometimes I'm in a train station without my luggage, which is still on the train I just got off. I usually wake up before I find out what happens.

After discussing the dream with friends, Jerry recognized two possible meanings. In both of them, the journey was his job. Although

continued on following page

resolved satisfactorily. Traveling on the wrong train may indicate your journey is in need of a correction. As with dreams of other modes of transportation, remember that the circumstances or activities of your dream trip might be more important than the destination itself.

treasure: A dream of a treasure might suggest a hidden talent or hidden abilities that you can now unearth. It could indicate latent psychic abilities.

tree: A tree is a symbol of strength and foundation. It can also symbolize inner strength. A tree exists both below the earth and above it. In that

continued from previous page
he didn't travel much, his work relied on making connections with sources for stories. His fear was that he wouldn't make contact with his sources or that when he reached them, he wouldn't be ready for the interview. His luggage represented his preparation for the interview.

The other interpretation involved the question of his future as a reporter. Jerry was tired of chasing down stories day after day and wanted to make a career change. But he feared that he was not prepared to make the change—that he would "miss his connection" to a new career.

sense, a tree transcends the sky above and the earth below and stands for the realms of nature and the spirit. To dream of a tree in new foliage represents a pleasant outcome to your hopes and desires.

tree climbing: Dreaming of climbing a tree might signify a quick ascent in business. Green trees newly felled augur unexpected unhappiness after a period of prosperity and delight.

trial: A dream of being on trial suggests that you are being judged, or you are afraid of being judged. Alternately, a trial in a dream could indicate that you are judging others too harshly.

triplets: To dream of triplets indicates success in a matter where failure was feared. For a man to dream of his wife having triplets represents a pleasing end to a situation that has long been in dispute. To hear newly born triplets crying suggests a disagreement that will soon be resolved in your favor.

tunnel: From a Freudian perspective, a dream of a tunnel suggests a vagina, and a train entering the tunnel represents sexual intercourse. A tunnel might also be a link between two conditions: When you exit the tunnel, you will enter a new state of mind.

turkey: To dream of a turkey indicates good luck will come your way, especially in business, where you might have abundant gains. To dream of eating turkey indicates you will be attending a happy, bounteous occasion—like a Thanksgiving celebration.

turtle or tortoise: While dreaming of a turtle might symbolize slow, painstaking movement, remember the story of "The Tortoise and the Hare," where slow and steady progress won the race. In this sense, turtles certainly symbolize the benefits of determined, calculated, and well-thought actions as opposed to hastiness. Be aware, therefore, of anything in your life that you might be in danger of blowing simply because you're rushing through it. This shelled creature is also a symbol of long life and spiritual development.

twins: A dream of twins could mean that there are two parts to a matter of concern or two aspects to your personality. Seeing twins in a dream symbolizes security in a business matter and faithfulness in a domestic issue.

UFO: The UFO reminds dreamers of their place as citizens of a very large universe.

umbrella: An umbrella represents protection against adverse conditions or an emotional flood from the unconscious. If the umbrella is closed and you're being soaked by a downpour, the indication is that you are open to your emotional needs.

uncle: If a man or woman dreams of an uncle, beware—sad news will soon reach you.

underground: To dream of being in an underground habitation often symbolizes contact with your subconscious. Other images in the dream will provide more meaning to the nature of the contact. Is there something you've been hiding here that should be brought to the "surface"? Ask yourself how you feel about the situation. Do you feel protected by the underground cavern or room? Or, are you being held prisoner or hiding? Dreaming of an underground railway could indicate passage to another state of being, a personal transformation. Examine the event of your life to see how such an interpretation would fit. (See also *basement*.)

underwear: A dream of underwear might symbolize that you are exposing something that is under cover or hidden. It could indicate that you're bringing matters from the unconscious to the surface.

unicorn: There are many stories about unicorns, the beautiful creatures of ancient mythology. These stories have been handed down from generation to generation among people of all countries, and this is a good dream to have. To dream of a unicorn means good fortune and happy circumstances will soon be yours.

unicycle: If you are riding a unicycle in a dream, it might be an indication that you are concerned about balance. Alternately, you're the "big wheel" and on your own.

United States: If you dream of the United States as a nation, such as taking a voyage to the United States, take care. Trouble might be around the corner.

United States mailbox: A mailbox is a symbol of authority; consequently, putting a letter in a mailbox might mean you are submitting to authority, or feeling guilt over a particular matter.

urination: A dream in which you urinate might simply indicate that you need to wake up and go to the bathroom. Symbolically, however, the dream could also indicate a desire to eliminate impurities from your life.

vagrant: Are you afraid of losing your home, stability, or livelihood? Perhaps you want to break away from social regimentation.

valuables: Uncovering valuables might symbolize the discovery of self-worth or inner resources.

vampire: To dream of a vampire might indicate that someone is draining energy from you or taking advantage of you. The message is to guard against people who take too much of your time or energy. To dream of battling or staking a vampire suggests a positive outcome versus someone with harmful intentions.

vault: A vault usually holds valuables. Your ability to open it determines the nature of the dream. If you hold the key, the vault could be a symbol of wealth and prosperity. If you are unable to open it, then the dream might signify that you are being frustrated in your effort to achieve wealth or a specific goal.

veil: A dream in which someone or something is veiled suggests that you're hiding something or something is being hidden from you.

velvet: If you dream of wearing velvet, this suggests good things will happen for you. You will be very successful in all your enterprises and it's possible that high honor will be conferred on you.

ventriloquist: If you dream of a ventriloquist, beware of deception and fraud. Dreaming of a ventriloquist can also mean that a love affair might turn out badly for you.

victim: A dream in which you are some sort of victim might indicate that you're feeling helpless regarding a situation. If someone rescues you, the dream suggests that help is available.

village: If you dream of places, it's best to dream of a village. To dream of a village means you will enjoy good health and will be provided for in your lifetime.

violin: A violin played in a dream portends a romantic interlude, a time of love and harmony. It can also mean that you or someone else is "high strung."

visitor: Encountering a visitor in a dream indicates that a new condition is entering your life. If you welcome the visitor, the change might be for the better. If you turn away the visitor, you're unwilling to change or you don't accept what is being offered.

volcano: The eruption of a volcano or a smoking volcano might suggest that your strong emotions are rising to the surface and need to be expressed before you literally explode.

vomit: To vomit in a dream might be a dramatic exhibition of a need to rid something or someone from your life. To dream of vomiting a chicken suggests an illness in a relative will be a cause of disappointment. To see others vomiting symbolizes that someone's false pretenses will soon be made apparent.

vulture: A dream that includes a vulture indicates that a predator is nearby.

wading: If you dream of wading in clear water expect joy. To dream of wading in muddy water, however, means that you will experience sorrow. For a young woman to dream of wading in clear water means she will have her heart's desire. And to dream of children wading signifies future happiness.

walking: A dream of walking in the woods means you will have business difficulties. Dreaming of walking at night means you will have struggle and difficulty. But dreaming of walking in pleasant places indicates good fortune and favor.

wallet: A wallet carries important items and personal effects, such as your identification, credit cards, money, and so on. It is also where you carry financial resources. If you dream of losing your wallet, it might relate to a concern about your sense of self or about your finances. What happens in the dream and how you react can help you determine its meaning. (See also *purse.*)

war: A dream of war could relate to reliving your past in the military. Whether you've served in the military or not, a dream of war might symbolize internal turmoil or a need to make peace with yourself, or others. By examining other elements in the dream, you might be able to determine the message behind the aggressive behavior. Since death is often imminent in war-torn situations, a dream that includes war images might also have to do with going through tough changes or transitions. (See also *death*.)

washing: If you are washing something in a dream, you might be attempting to cleanse or purify the self. If a stain won't come out, the dream could relate to a concern about something from your past connected with feelings of guilt.

watch: A dream of a watch pertains to the passing of time. (See also *clock*.)

water: A dream of water can relate to the emotions or the unconscious. In the Freudian perspective, water relates to sexual matters, usually the female genitalia. Water is also sometimes interpreted to represent the source of life or a spiritual journey. Dreaming of water can be an indication of good health, as well. (See also *lake*, *ocean*, *river*, and *waves*.)

waterfall: Water signifies the unconscious or the emotions, so to dream of waterfalls might represent a sudden or dramatic change in the dreamer's emotional state.

waves: Waves symbolize the power of the unconscious or emotions. Enormous breaking waves might represent powerful emotions, and gentle waves might suggest a tranquil state of mind.

weapon: Weapons may stand for the male genitals. The meaning of a dream that includes weapons is best determined by considering who is holding the weapon and how it is being used.

web: A web signifies the intertwining of all things. It represents life's network where everything from the smallest neutron to the largest galaxy is connected, including your life.

wedding: Weddings are a union between two people, and dreams of weddings might symbolize the joining or acceptance of your unconscious to an idea or emotion. To attend a wedding in a dream connotes an occasion that might bring about bitterness and delayed success. To dream of a wedding that is not approved by your parents suggests unrest among family members over a situation.

wedding license: If you should dream of such practical wedding matters as a marriage license, this doesn't denote easy times ahead. You might make an unhappy alliance and find your pride humiliated.

weeds: Dreaming of weeds suggests that something needs to be weeded out from your life. An overgrown garden might signify that something is being neglected in your life. If you dream of tangled weeds, that is indicative of a need for cleansing or purification.

well: A well in a dream reveals that resources are available deep within you, although you might not be aware of it. To fall into a well symbolizes a loss of control regarding a matter at hand. A dry well indicates that you feel a part of your life is empty and needs to be nourished. To draw water from a well denotes the fulfillment of ardent desires.

wet: As in the saying, "you're all wet," wetness represents uncertainty or a lack of knowledge. Maybe someone is giving you bad advice for a particular situation. For a young woman to dream that she is soaking wet symbolizes a disgraceful affair with someone who is already attached.

whale: A whale is an enormous mammal and to dream of one might indicate that you are dealing with a whale of a project. On the other hand, a whale dream might suggest you are overwhelmed. Whales can also relate to water and the relationship of the self to the unconscious and the emotions. Another possible interpretation might be related to a journey—physical or spiritual—that aids enlightenment. Whales can also symbolize regeneration.

whirlpool: Water represents the emotions or the unconscious, so to dream of a whirlpool might indicate that your emotions are in a state of flux and can ensnarl you unless caution is exercised.

whirlwind: A dream of a whirlwind suggests that you are confronting a change in a matter at hand that threatens to overwhelm you. Pay attention to the other aspects of the dream. Are you facing this danger alone or with somebody? Are you in your house?

wife: The husband-wife relationship is of key significance, and as is the case with dreams of husbands, a dream of your wife usually arises out of issues related to ups and downs of everyday life. The dreamer's own feelings and the general atmosphere of the dream often speak to whether it's positive or negative. If positive images or events are involved in your dream of your wife, it probably bodes well. However, if negative events or images are involved, it might be signifying your own fears or concerns. (Although this does not necessarily mean they are true-to-life fact.) (See also *husband*.)

will: If you dream of a will or of making your will, it's possible that momentous trials and speculations will occur in your life.

willow tree: Dreaming of a willow indicates you will soon make a sad journey and be consoled by your friends.

wind: Dreaming of wind softly blowing signifies you will receive a considerable inheritance from a beloved one. Although you experience sadness over the death of this loved one, you will know happiness in the future.

If you dream you are walking against a brisk wind, it indicates you are courageous, resist temptations, and pursue your hopes with a plucky determination. You will be successful. If, however, in your dream the wind blows you along against your wishes, it signifies you might have disappointments in love and in business.

window: If a window appears in a dream, it might symbolize a view of your life from the inside out. Are there changes you would like to make? If the view is illuminated, then the outlook is bright. If you are on the outside looking in, you might feel that you have been excluded from something.

wine: Drinking wine in a dream can be a sign of celebration. It can also represent an elevated or altered state of mind. In a spiritual sense, wine might symbolize a transformation. For an alcoholic or someone who has been affected by one, wine or other alcoholic beverages can represent a negative influence.

wine cellar: If you dream you are in a wine cellar, it's good news. You will share in profits, although the profits could come from a doubtful source. If you dream you are in a wine cellar drinking wine—watch out—you might wake up in the morning with a hangover.

wings: Wings are a means of transport and they might suggest that you will soar to wealth and honor, or that you are worried over someone who has gone on a long journey.

winter: Winter is often synonymous with the yearly death of nature, after its three seasons of regeneration, growth, and harvest. Winter is also a time for hibernation or slowing down. If you dream of winter, consider if you have recently gone through any sort of metaphoric death. Have you recently ended a relationship or put a bad situation or habit behind you?

witch: How one sees a witch determines the meaning of a dream in which one appears. The Halloween image of a witch might be symbolic of a scary or evil scenario. For those involved in Wicca or attracted to New Age ideas, a witch might relate to the worship and respect of nature and the earth.

wolf: In Native American lore, the wolf is good medicine, a symbol of the pathfinder, a teacher with great wisdom and knowledge. Dreaming of a wolf can be auspicious. Alternately, the wolf can be a symbol of a lone male aggressively pursuing a young female as in the Little Red Riding Hood fable.

woman: The appearance of different types of women can symbolize different things in a dream. A dark-haired woman with blue eyes and a pug nose may represent a withdrawal from a matter at hand. A brown-eyed woman with a hook nose may suggest that you will be lured into a speculative venture. A woman who appears with auburn hair only adds to your anxiety over an issue. A blonde woman is symbolic of a favorable or pleasing outcome.

woodpecker: This bird indicates that a change in literal or figurative weather is on the horizon.

writing: Writing is usually difficult to read in a dream, so the message is usually symbolic. Writing can serve as a warning, as in "the handwriting is on the wall." Writing could also suggest that your inner self is seeking to make contact with your conscious self. Ancient writings in a dream indicate that the dreamer is seeking knowledge from the distant past.

yard: Dreaming of a yard might relate to your childhood, to a time when you played in it. The dream might symbolize a longing for a care-free time, for more personal space, or for something to fill the vacancy of the yard.

yellow: In the positive sense, yellow is the symbol of brightness, energy, and intellect. The color can also be linked to cowardly behavior.

youth: A dream of a youth might signify that you are being energized by those younger than you. Seeing yourself as younger in a dream might point to youthful self-empowerment.

Z

zebra: Dreaming of zebras running fast on the hoof indicates you are interested in fleeting enterprises. If you dream of a zebra wild in its native environment, you might pursue a fancy that could bring unsatisfactory results. Beware of those with multicolored stripes!

zero: A symbol of many interpretations, zero can mean emptiness, a lack of something in your life. It also forms a circle and can stand for wholeness and completion, or even the mysteries of the unknown. In Freudian terms, the shape is reminiscent of a vagina and suggests a desire for sexual relations.

zoo: A dream of a zoo might relate to a feeling of being in a cage. It could also symbolize chaos as in "The place is like a zoo." Alternately, it could recall a time of recreation, relaxation, and pleasure.

Appendix A

Sleep- and Dream-Related Organizations, Publications, and Web Sites

Following is a list of organizations and publications involved in dream-related activities, if you are interested in pursuing additional information as you continue with your dream work.

Alfred Adler Institute
594 Broadway
New York, NY 10012
Phone: (212) 254-1048
Web site: *www.alfredadler-ny.org*
e-mail: *alfredadler@ny.com*

One of the first psychoanalytic training institutes in New York, the Alfred Adler Institute provides postgraduate training in psychotherapy and counseling rooted in the theories of Austrian psychiatrist Alfred Adler. A contemporary of Sigmund Freud, Adler's views differed in that his humanistic theories of motivation set him apart from Freud's biological approach, and his theory of individual psychology took each person's uniqueness into greater consideration.

American Sleep Association (ASA)

614 South 8th St., Suite 282
Philadelphia, PA 19147
Phone: (443) 593-2285
Web site: *www.americansleepassociation.org*
e-mail: for general questions, *sleep@1sleep.com*

The national affiliation of The International Sleep Medicine Association, The American Sleep Association is the first organization related to sleep health and sleep disorders to link people all over North America. The ASA provides a wealth of help and information on insomnia, night terrors, narcolepsy, and many other sleep-related disorders. You can also find information on other related organizations and the ASA's journal on its Web site.

American Society for Psychical Research (ASPR)

5 West 73rd St.
New York, NY 10023
Phone: (212) 799-5050
Web site: *www.aspr.com*
e-mail: *aspr@aspr.com*

The oldest psychical research organization in the United States, The ASPR was founded in 1885 by a group of scholars looking to explore the realms of human consciousness. (This group included renowned Harvard psychologist and Professor of Philosophy, William James.) The ASPR supports the scientific investigation of psychic and paranormal phenomena, including the telepathic influences on dreams. Information on the newsletter and journal of the ASPR can be obtained through its Web site.

Association for Research and Enlightenment (A.R.E.)

215 67th St.
Virginia Beach, VA 23451
Phone: (800) 333-4499
Web site: *www.edgarcayce.org*
e-mail: *are@edgarcayce.org*

A.R.E., also known as the Edgar Cayce Foundation, is the international headquarters for the work of famed psychic Edgar Cayce, who was able to experience his insights through a self-induced sleep state. A.R.E. offers an extensive research library based on Cayce's recorded readings and provides year-round seminars on a wide range of topics related to parapsychology, including dreams. The Web site provides information on the association's group activities, as well as links to other Edgar Cayce Centers around the world.

Association for the Study of Dreams (ASD)

Information Office
P.O. Box 1166
Orinda, CA 94563
Phone: (925) 258-1822
Web site: *www.asdreams.org*
e-mail: *asdreams@aol.com*

ASD provides an international forum for promoting research and dispensing information about the psychological and therapeutic aspects of dreams and their interpretation. The association sponsors conferences and offers *Dreaming,* a multidisciplinary journal devoted specifically to dreams, as well as *Dream Time*, a magazine that serves as an information service and forum for ASD members.

Atlantic University

215 67th St.

Virginia Beach, VA 23451-2061

Phone: (800) 428-1512

Web site: *www.atlanticuniv.org*

e-mail: *registrar@atlanticuniv.edu*

Atlantic University, an outgrowth of A.R.E., offers an accredited M.A. degree in transpersonal psychology as well as a wide range of at-home study courses or on-site courses in Virginia Beach. Information on admissions; tuition, fees and financial aid; and faculty can be found on the Web site.

Cleargreen, Inc.

10812A Washington Blvd.

Culver City, CA 90232

Phone: (310) 839-7150

Web site: *www.cleargreen.com*

e-mail: Readers can send e-mail questions through Cleargreen's Web site's Contact Information page.

Cleargreen was founded by Carlos Castaneda and his colleagues to promote the teachings of Don

Juan Matus, a Mexican Indian shaman who taught dreaming techniques to Castaneda. Matus's techniques involve practices that allow humans to perceive energy directly as it flows into the universe, without having to turn that energy into sensory data in the typical sense. The organization promotes seminars in which these "magical passes," called Tensegrity, are taught. Cleargreen publishes a newsletter, *Infinity: A Journal of Applied Hermeneutics*, and links to information on this journal, as well as workshops, classes, practice groups, books, and videos, can be found on the Web site.

Common Boundary

4905 Del Ray Avenue, Suite 210
Bethesda, MD 20814
Phone: (301) 652-9495
Web site: *www.commonboundary.org*
e-mail: *connect@commonboundary.org*

Common Boundary is a nonprofit educational organization founded to foster support and communication for those in mental health, helping, and healing professions, and anyone interested in the interrelationships between psychology, spirituality, and creativity. It publishes an award-winning bimonthly magazine and holds annual conferences.

Dream Network

1137 Powerhouse Ln. Suite 22

Moab, UT 84532

Phone: (435) 259-5936

Web site: *www.dreamnetwork.net*

e-mail: *Publisher@DreamNetwork.net*

Dream Network offers a quarterly journal devoted to exploring the relationship between dreams and myths. Its stated purpose is to "demystify dream work and to integrate dream-sharing into our lives for the enhancement of our culture." The Network's Web site offers an online e-zine, as well as information and links regarding ongoing dream groups and dream sharing.

C.G. Jung Foundation for Analytical Psychology

28 E. 39th St.

New York, NY 10016-2587

Phone: 1-800-356-JUNG

Web site: *www.cgjungny.org*

e-mail: *info@cgjungfoundationny.org*

The Jung Foundation offers training and information on analytical psychology based on Jungian concepts. It hosts an extensive roster of public lectures, seminars, courses, symposia, and workshops.

The foundation publishes a journal, *Quadrant*, and its archival material includes studies on archetypal symbolism. The Web site provides details regarding workshops, summer study programs, continuing education, and more.

National Sleep Foundation

1522 K Street, NW, Suite 500
Washington, DC 20005
Phone: (202) 347-3471
Web site: *www.sleepfoundation.org*
e-mail: *nsf@sleepfoundation.org*

The National Sleep Foundation is an independent, nonprofit organization that promotes education on sleep disorders, develops community resources, sponsors educational and research programs, and encourages local support groups. The Foundation publishes *Sleep Matters*, a quarterly news magazine.

Omega Institute

150 Lake Drive
Rhinebeck, NY 12572
Phone: (800) 944-1001
Web site: *www.eomega.org*
e-mail: *registration@eomega.org*

The Omega Institute is a holistic education center that is well respected for its work in a variety of disciplines, including holistic health, meditation, yoga, transformational psychology, and spirituality. It offers workshops and seminars taught by leaders in psychology, metaphysics, shamanism, the arts, and other related fields. Information on registration and free catalogs can be obtained through the Web site's home page.

The Pacific Northwest Center for Dream Studies
219 First Avenue S, Suite 405
Seattle, WA 98104
Phone: (206) 447-1895

The Pacific Northwest Center offers dream work classes and psychotherapy using Jungian, Gestalt, and Delaney methods as well as ceremonial art forms.

The Saybrook Institute
450 Pacific, 3rd Fl.
San Francisco, CA 94123
Phone: (415) 433-9200
Web site: *www.saybrook.edu*
e-mail: *admissions@saybrook.edu*

Founded and directed by Dr. Stanley Krippner, a renowned dream researcher and author, Saybrook is an accredited graduate school that offers a curriculum focused on humanistic psychology and human science. It provides students with many opportunities to study dreams. Write for more information.

Sleep Research Society (SRS)

c/o Cleveland Clinic S-51
Dept. of Neurology
9500 Euclid Ave.
Cleveland, OH 44195 Illinois
Phone: SRS: (708) 492-0930;
         Cleveland Clinic: (216) 444-9083
Web site: *www.sleepresearchsociety.org/site*
e-mail: *jwrabetz@aasmnet.org*

SRS conducts research into the study of sleep, and it promotes and disseminates information on the physiological and psychological aspects of sleep. Its journal, *Sleep,* is published bimonthly.

Appendix B

Books on Dreaming

If you are looking for more insights into any of the dream types or techniques discussed in this book, the titles below are a good place to start.

Ball, P., *10,000 Dreams Interpreted*. New York, Gramercy Books, 1996.

Castaneda, C., *The Art of Dreaming*. New York, HarperCollins, 1993.

Dalfen, L., *Dreams Do Come True*. Avon, MA, Adams Media. Out of print.

Delaney, G., *Breakthrough Dreaming: How to Tap the Power of Your 24-Hour Mind*. New York, Bantam, 1991.

Faraday, A., *Dream Power*. New York, Afar Publishers, 1972.

Faraday, A., *The Dream Game*. New York, Harper & Row, 1974.

Garfield, P., *Creative Dreaming*. New York, Ballantine, 1974.

Godwin, M., *The Lucid Dreamer*. New York, Simon & Schuster, 1994.

González-Wippler, M., *Dreams and What They Mean to You*. St. Paul, MN, Llewellyn Publications, 2001.

Harner, M., *The Way of the Shaman*. New York, Harper & Row, 1980.

Innes, B., *The Book of Dreams*. New York, Brown Packaging Books Ltd., 2000.

Jung, C., *Man and His Symbols*. New York, Dell, 1964.

Jung, C., *Memories, Dreams, Reflections*. New York, Vintage, 1961.

LaBerge, S., *Lucid Dreaming*. New York, Ballantine, 1986.

LaBerge, S. and Rheingold, H., *Exploring the World of Lucid Dreaming*. New York, Random House, 1990.

Lewis, J., *The Dream Encyclopedia*. Detroit, Visible Ink Books, 1995.

Mallon, M., *The Dream Bible*. Cincinnati, OH, Walking Stick Press, 2003.

Maxmen, J., *A Good Night's Sleep*. New York, Warner, 1981.

McGuire, W. and Hull, R. (Eds.), *C.G. Jung Speaking*. Princeton, NJ, Princeton University Press, 1977.

Michaels, S., *The Bedside Guide to Dreams*. New York, Fawcett Crest, 1995.

Miller, G. H., *10,000 Dreams Interpreted*. Barnes and Noble Books, 1997.

Morris, J., *The Dream Workbook*. New York, Fawcett Crest, 1985.

Perkins, J., *PsychoNavigation*. Rochester, VT, Destiny Books, 1990.

Perkins, J., *The World as You Dream It: Shamanic Teachings from the Amazon and Andes*. Rochester, VT, Destiny Books, 1994.

Robinson, S. and Corbett, T., *The Complete Dreamer's Dictionary*. New York, Warner Books, 1974.

Sanford, J., *Dreams and Healing: A Succinct and Lively Interpretation of Dreams*. New York, Paulist Press, 1978.

Telesco, P., *The Language of Dreams*. Berkeley, CA, Crossing Press, 1997.

Ullman, M., Krippner, S., and Vaughan, A., *Dream Telepathy*. Toronto, Macmillan, 1973.

Ullman, M. and Zimmerman, N., *Working with Dreams*. New York, Dell, 1979.

Villoldo, A., *Dance of the Four Winds*. New York, Harper & Row, 1990.

Villoldo, A., *Island of the Sun: Mastering the Inca Medicine Wheel*. San Francisco, HarperSanFrancisco, 1992.

Williams, S., *Jungian-Senoi Dreamwork Manual*. Berkeley, Journal Press, 1980.

Index